The Hog in the 21st Century

Phillip and Robert King

B.T. Batsford • London

First published 1999

© Phillip and Robert King 1999

ISBN 0 7134 8297 4

A CIP catalogue record for this book is available from the British Library.

Typeset by KEATS, Harrow on the Hill

Printed by Creative Print & Design, Ebbw Vale, Wales
for the publishers,
B. T. Batsford, 9 Blenheim Court, Brewery Road
London N7 9NT
A member of the Chrysalis Group plc

CONTENTS

INTRODUCTION

Victor Mollo's famous Menagerie was conceived nearly forty years ago. Its wildly eccentric inhabitants belonged to a bridge club called *The Griffins*. As a test for prospective members, Victor devised a catechism:

> "Is bridge a medium through which you like to express yourself? Do the cards, leaving the humdrum world behind, take you to a place where you can be bold and brilliant, resolute and resourceful, clever, calculating and cunning? Does playing well give you a glow of satisfaction? Does playing badly make you squirm?"

Four yesses proved that you were at heart a Griffin. Then came the prospectus:

> "The members of this exclusive club differ from lesser mortals only in being more colourful, more vibrant, more clearly defined in all their traits, good and bad. They have the same frailties, commit the same follies and are just as comic in their vanity and their pretensions as the rest of the human race."

In including them in the human race he was doing them less than justice. Most Griffins proudly bear the name of the animals or birds they resemble, which has the delicious effect of making them more than human.

Occasionally, we meet visitors who actually work for a living; keyhole manufacturers, morticians, and unpublished authors. But we suspect that the only occupation of the members is to contribute to the government's unemployment statistics, which they do with great distinction. This is as it should be, for few of them are even remotely employable.

Yet all the Griffins seem to be comfortably off. They can afford not only to lose large sums to the Hideous Hog, but to keep him and themselves on a diet of Beluga caviar, Colchester oysters and Aylesbury ducklings. Their champagne is never Tesco's own label, and their port is invariably of a noble vintage.

They do not appear to have much of a life away from the club. Occasionally they are interrupted by a telephone call so urgent that it causes them to play a correct card. They have been known to leave a rubber unfinished, in order to be on time for an engagement two hours previously. They sometimes mention cousins, nephews and aunts, but the Griffins themselves appear to be unmarried, unattached and unencumbered, which, as we get to know them, becomes unsurprising.

One thing is surprising. The more we learn about their fads and foibles, the fonder of them we grow. This is a tribute to Victor Mollo's skill, for he wished it so. Even the fearsome Secretary Bird has a tiny nook in our affections, and many a tear will be shed when he finally joins the Great Laws and Ethics Committee in the Sky.

But of course he never will; like all the Griffins, he is immune to the ravages of time, character development and carbon dating. He and they will still be around to celebrate the fourth millennium.

If the Devil does not desert me, I shall await the Millennium in pleasurable anticipation. My addictions will see me through.

Victor Mollo
Confessions of an Addict

THE CAST

H.H.

A Rabelaisian creation, H.H. has a gargantuan appetite for high-stake bridge and high calorie nourishment. Easily the best player in the club, he is regarded as a towering genius, and cannot understand why he is so grossly underrated. Aptly named the Hideous Hog, he modestly prefers to be known by his initials.

Papa

What Papa lacks in success, he makes up for in brilliance, and is never afraid to admit it. A superb and subtle technician, he has been known to false card with a singleton, and hopes one day to develop the knack of false-carding with a void. His other ambition is to convince the other Griffins that the Hog is the club's *second* best player.

Karapet

Karapet Djoulikyan, the Free Armenian, is the unluckiest mortal since the man who bet ten thousand shekels on Goliath. He always expects the worst and is rarely disappointed. Nothing can shake his indomitable will to lose, and nothing can empty a room faster than his hard luck stories.

R.R.

In contrast, the Rueful Rabbit is supernaturally lucky. He used to think of himself as the second worst player on the planet ... until he met the Toucan. Seldom capable of playing the right card until trick thirteen, he is rescued time and again by his Guardian Angel, who is the best in the business. Whenever R.R. perpetrates a fatuous misplay, the G.A. transforms it into a masterstroke.

T.T.

On a scale of 0-10, Timothy the Toucan scores minus twelve for arrogance. Desperately seeking affection, he ingratiates himself by apologising for every mistake before he makes it. He never misses a chance to congratulate his partners when they bring off a coup which is beyond his ability, such as a finesse.

W.W.

A retired accountant since early youth, Walter the Walrus believes that making a contract without the regulation values is a pernicious form of grand larceny. He claims the Milton Work Point Count as one of the Seven Wonders of the Modern World. Signalling also makes the list. At number nine.

S.B.

The Emeritus Professor of Bio-Sophistry, alias the Secretary Bird, is the club's self-appointed judge, jury and executioner. His approach to bridge is based on two unshakeable beliefs:

1. Observing the laws of the game is more important than playing it.
2. Judge Jeffries was a wimp.

C.C.

If he lives to be a hundred, as many members fear he will, Colin the Corgi will always be known as the facetious young man from Oxbridge, and a future bridge master. In his ability to make lesser players feel insignificant he has already achieved expert status.

Ch.Ch.

An incurable chatterbox, Charlie the Chimp loves to discuss every hand except the one he is playing. When he cannot win by sharp practice or downright chicanery, he is capable of reaching the dizzy heights of mediocrity, from which he can look down on the Rabbit, the Toucan and the Walrus.

O.O.

As the Griffins' Senior Kibitzer, Oscar the Owl has acquired awesome powers. Young kibitzers come from far and wide to learn their craft under his stern gaze. Had the demands of his career allowed him time to play the game, he might have attained master rank.

P.P.

Peregrine the Penguin is Oscar's opposite number at the Unicorns, and it was under his tutorship that Walter the Walrus became the player he is. Despite this, Peregrine is always a respected visitor to the Griffins.

M.M.

Molly the Mule, one of the stars of the all female Mermaids Club, was the first member of the stronger sex to become a regular visitor to the Griffins. Radiating goodwill to all humankind except the male half, she makes up for her undistinguished play by her invincibility in the post-mortem.

D.D.

Dolly the Dove's gentle manner and soft cooing voice when she doubles her opponents into game make her one of the most sought after opponents in the Western Hemisphere. For nine consecutive years she was voted the Mermaids' most promising newcomer.

The Squirrel

The Squirrel is Mrs Victor Mollo, who used to "wear the pencil, wield the scissors and read the proofs with a rod of iron" for her husband. She does not appear in this book, but the fact that it has been published is due to her kindness and encouragement.

Chapter 1

The Rabbit Takes Charge

As he gazed proudly at his new Turkish Rolex, the Rueful Rabbit noticed that there were only seventy-two shopping days to the Millennium. Never having witnessed the dawn of a new century, he wondered if any of his fellow Griffins had done so.

The most likely candidate was Oscar the Owl, who was rumoured to be in his eighties, but it took the Rabbit only five minutes to calculate that to live during three consecutive centuries, a man would have to be at least ninety-two.

Trembling with excitement, the Rabbit realised that for the first time in his undistinguished life, he was on an equal footing with the Hog, Papa and the other eminent Griffins: at midnight on the 31st December, they too would be taking a step into the unknown.

How could he exploit this unprecedented lack of disadvantage? After a few minutes of fruitless pondering, he wandered into the card room, hoping for inspiration.

R.R. was a poor kibitzer. Even when playing a contract, his attention span was woefully brief: when watching the game it was minuscule. His demeanour was more rueful than ever as he sat down to watch his friend, Timothy the Toucan, attempt to bring home a four heart contract.

A student would have learned very little from the play, but a great deal about the exhilarating nature of bridge with the Griffins.

East/West Game. Dealer South.

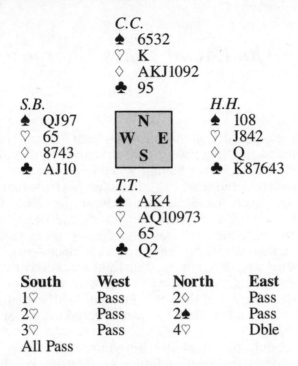

C.C.
♠ 6532
♡ K
◇ AKJ1092
♣ 95

S.B.
♠ QJ97
♡ 65
◇ 8743
♣ AJ10

H.H.
♠ 108
♡ J842
◇ Q
♣ K87643

T.T.
♠ AK4
♡ AQ10973
◇ 65
♣ Q2

South	West	North	East
1♡	Pass	2◇	Pass
2♡	Pass	2♠	Pass
3♡	Pass	4♡	Dble
All Pass			

The Hog's double was tactical. T.T.'s dummy play was usually worth a trick to the defence. When he was rattled, it was worth two or three. The Emeritus Professor of Bio-Sophistry, unaffectionately known as the Secretary Bird, led the ♠Q, and Timothy thanked Colin the Corgi warmly. When the dummy went down, he thanked him again.

"More than I deserve, partner," he said. "But I wish you were playing it."

"So does he," muttered the Hog, in a whisper so inaudible that it produced a peal of laughter from only three tables.

The Toucan captured the queen with his ace and, playing at the top of his form, avoided making an error until trick two, when, tabling a trump with trembling fingers, he suddenly noticed that it was the ace. "I'm so sorry," he said, desperately attempting to withdraw it.

"Too late," snapped S.B., covering sadistically with his five.

"The rules of the game are quite explicit. It's a pity more people do not trouble to learn them."

"Come, Professor," remonstrated H.H. "Surely you wouldn't wish to take advantage of a trivial lapse by an old friend. Take back your ace, Timothy."

"Respect for the law is the foundation of civilised society," pontificated S.B., his pince-nez gleaming perilously, while wild tufts of hair protruded at right-angles from his ears.

"Oh dear," cried Timothy. "I didn't mean to cause ... Play the king please, Colin."

When T.T. continued with the queen and ten of hearts, H.H., fuming impotently, took the trick and returned a spade to declarer's king. The Toucan captured, drew the outstanding trump, and agonised over his next move. Suddenly he remembered an expert safety play. He advanced a diamond and rose with dummy's ace, in case the Hog held a singleton queen.

It was only then that he saw that there was no way of returning to hand to repeat the finesse. Halfway through his abject apology to the Corgi, he bounced in his seat when the Hog's ◊Q appeared, and began an equally abject apology to his opponents as he gathered in two doubled overtricks.

The Hog was choleric with rage. His return of a spade, rather than the obvious club, had been masterly. By removing the Toucan's entry, he had prevented declarer from testing diamonds in the normal fashion. With no way of getting back to hand, a sane declarer would have finessed the first round of diamonds. But why blame the defenceless Timothy when there was a juicier victim awaiting sentence? He glared venomously at S.B.

"Why didn't you let Timothy take back his ace and commit *felo de se*?" he jeered. "He would have led a trump to the king, returned to hand with a spade, played off two top trumps and discovered the bad news. Now, when he plays on diamonds I could ruff the second round and we would cash a spade and two clubs."

S.B. hissed in several arcane languages. "Better to fail through upholding the law than to succeed by flouting it," he pontificated. "It would be like profiting from a crime."

"Well, if you're so set against crime, Professor, kindly stop stabbing your partner in the back."

"He can't help it," quipped Colin the Corgi, who had been savouring every moment of the conflict. "S.B. is a legend in his own knifetime."

The Rabbit sat in rapt admiration. He had not understood a single word of the Hog's analysis, but he knew that Timothy, aided by S.B., had proved yet again that the humblest player could topple the mightiest master, just as David had toppled Goliath, or George Washington had toppled his father's cherry tree. Suddenly he knew how the Griffins should mark the Millennium. He squared his round shoulders and prepared for Leadership.

Oozing purpose from every pore, he made his way to the bar, where Oscar was enjoying a pre-prandial sherry. "Oscar," he proclaimed, "we must do something about the Millennium."

"I agree," blinked the Senior Kibitzer. "But I'm afraid it's too late to stop it."

It was also too late to stop the Rabbit. "You could be right, Oscar. But people are bringing out all sorts of lists, like the Hundred Best U.S. Presidents, and I thought, er, that is to say, it occurred to me ..."

"If you are suggesting that we compile a list of the Hundred Best Played Hands, the Hog has already done so," stated O.O. "Including the dates on which he played them."

"No, Oscar," protested the Rabbit. "What I meant was... well, we're always hearing about the Hog and Papa and Colin, and how clever they are, and they're quite right to tell us so, so we don't mind them winning our money, but where would they be without Timothy or Walter or the rest of us, er ... ordinary players?"

"My dear R.R.," soothed the Owl. "Your many admirers describe your unique talents with a variety of epithets, not all of them unprintable, but never as ordinary. Yet I take your point. History honours Archimedes for leaping out of his bath, reciting his Principle, and crying 'Eureka!' But it ignores that unsung host of nonentities who only cried 'Where's the soap?' The Millennium provides us with an opportunity to redress the balance. We shall reward Molly the Mule, S.B., Charlie the Chimp –"

Pieces of Eight

His eloquence was deflated by the arrival of Colin the Corgi, the facetious young man from Oxbridge, and a perennially rising star of the London bridge firmament. He possessed the essential expert qualities of acid wit, when ridiculing the errors of his partners, and deep compassion, when excusing his own. By now, Colin's future was well behind him, but his past was full of rich promise.

"I'm glad you're here, C.C.," said Oscar. "To celebrate the Millennium R.R. has generously offered to donate glittering prizes for remarkable card play."

"Really?" The Corgi raised a cynical eyebrow. "That is the most disinterested suggestion I have heard since the Hog sponsored a slimmer of the month award."

The Rabbit had never been able to penetrate the subtle layers of the Corgi's fourth form humour. Why shouldn't H.H. sponsor a slimming competition? The less everyone else consumed, the more there would be for him. He pictured the Hog, gobbling up other people's canapés and drinks as though they were doubled overtricks ...

"Actually R.R. has envisaged some more unusual contests." The Owl beamed paternally at the blushing Rabbit. "He suggests that we recognise qualities other than that overrated virtue, skill."

"That's it exactly!" The Rabbit bubbled with excitement. He was a modest fellow, with every reason to be so, but he knew that when skill was removed from the equation, he could slug toe-to-toe with the best. "Flair, for example," he ventured hopefully.

"Of course," sniffed Colin. "Flair is your euphemism for sheer blind luck. Did you tell Oscar about your bizarre spade game yesterday?"

"Yes," lied the Owl, but he was a microsecond too late. C.C. had already begun the inevitable sketch:

Game All. Dealer North.

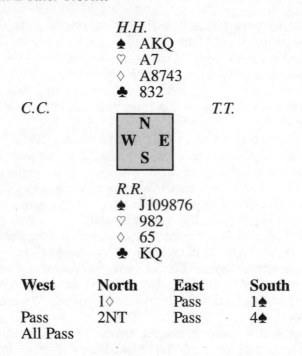

H.H.
♠ AKQ
♡ A7
◇ A8743
♣ 832

C.C.   *T.T.*

R.R.
♠ J109876
♡ 982
◇ 65
♣ KQ

West	North	East	South
	1◇	Pass	1♠
Pass	2NT	Pass	4♠
All Pass			

"A glance at the diagram will tell you why the Hog was unable to right-side the contract," said the Corgi. "So imagine yourself at the helm in four spades, Oscar. Naturally, I found the annoying lead of a trump, so I defy you to make ten tricks."

Oscar bristled. Due to a split vote by the committee, it was not a capital offence to defy the Senior Kibitzer. The maximum penalty was a stiff term of penal solitude, during which nobody would kibitz, or discuss hands with, the offender. But the kindly Owl chose the marginally lesser punishment of telling C.C. how to make the contract.

"I will win in dummy," he smiled, noting the vigorous nod of approval from the Rabbit. "Then I will wait stoically for the Toucan's discard."

The Rabbit gasped. "How do you know he discarded?" he squeaked.

"If trumps break two-two, the contract is Rab- I mean foolproof," declared the Owl. "If they are three-one, I have an

excellent chance of setting up diamonds. And Colin is too much
of a gentleman to insult me with a simple problem." He studied
the hand for a full minute, then bowed his head in defeat.

"Giving up so soon?" the Corgi taunted him.

"My only real hope is to ruff a heart on the table," retorted
Oscar. "Continuing to assume the worst, I expect to find you
with the heart king and the club ace, convenient entries to
remove dummy's trumps."

"Correct," nodded the Corgi sadistically.

"Yet evidently R.R. succeeded," mused the Owl. "But how?"

The Rabbit was acutely embarrassed. It seemed churlish to
shame a man who had kibitzed a million deals and played nearly
a dozen, but that was one of the penalties of leadership.

"I, er, thought I'd start on the clubs," he began. "Of course
I'm not such a clever card reader as you, so I was hoping that
Timothy had the ace, but Colin had it, and he played a second
trump. Then I called for dummy's small heart. I thought
Timothy might go up with the king, if he had it, thinking I had
the queen, if he didn't have it, only I was wrong on both counts,
and Colin cleverly overtook the ten with his king and drew
dummy's last trump."

As R.R. paused for breath and a therapeutic gulp of cherry
brandy, Oscar's mind raced, but he couldn't spot a winning line,
even when the Corgi had filled in the East/West cards:

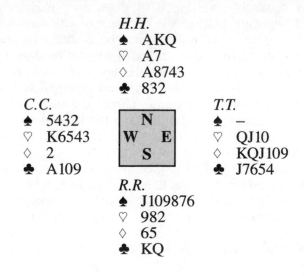

```
                     H.H.
                     ♠ AKQ
                     ♡ A7
                     ◊ A8743
                     ♣ 832
      C.C.                             T.T.
      ♠ 5432          ┌─────────┐      ♠ —
      ♡ K6543         │   N     │      ♡ QJ10
      ◊ 2             │ W   E   │      ◊ KQJ109
      ♣ A109          │   S     │      ♣ J7654
                      └─────────┘
                     R.R.
                     ♠ J109876
                     ♡ 982
                     ◊ 65
                     ♣ KQ
```

"Where was I?" wondered the Rabbit. "Oh, yes, well I got back to hand with the queen of clubs, and led out a lot of trumps – I forget how many, but I know I had one left. I've seen the Hog rattle out long suits, and everyone seems to make mistakes – it's easy enough to do, you know, I sometimes make them myself. And they must have made some this time, because I only had nine tricks, yet I made ten."

Sketching rapidly, C.C. smoothly took up the narrative. "This was the position after the fifth trump had been played," he showed them.

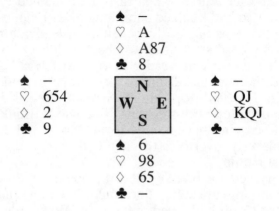

```
              ♠  –
              ♡  A
              ◇  A87
              ♣  8
♠  –                        ♠  –
♡  654      ┌─────────┐     ♡  QJ
◇  2        │    N    │     ◇  KQJ
♣  9        │ W     E │     ♣  –
            │    S    │
            └─────────┘
              ♠  6
              ♡  98
              ◇  65
              ♣  –
```

"After crossing to the ace of diamonds, R.R. applied all twelve of his brain cells to the problem of calculating whether the eight of clubs was good. When he decided to lead it, the Toucan was in deadly peril, though I'm sure he didn't know it. If he threw a diamond, a half-awake declarer would ruff and set up a diamond trick in dummy, and even R.R., with his legendary, er, flair … Anyway, Timothy randomly chose the apparently lesser evil of relinquishing the jack of hearts."

"I must remember to congratulate him," cried the Rabbit. "I had no idea he'd worked it out so cleverly."

Oscar began to see the light. He blinked his round amber eyes twice. He was about to blink them a third time when the Corgi, who deplored physical excess, came to his rescue.

"R.R. groaned when I won with my club nine," resumed Colin. "But I had nothing to lead but those small hearts. Back on the table with the ace, he led a diamond and ruffed. And I'll say this for him: he had the grace to blush when his eight of hearts won the last trick."

He waited to allow a coterie of Oscar's trainees, who had been kibitzing the conversation, to burst into spontaneous applause. O.O. raised an imperious finger, the acclamation ceased, and the Rabbit's blush stopped halfway up his long pointed ears."

"The Hog described it as an elementary combination trump squeeze," commented the Corgi. "I call it sheer, blind luck." [1]

"Well, perhaps I'm not as bad as certain people think I am," claimed R.R. "If my eight of clubs didn't turn out to be a winner, it was only fair that my eight of hearts did. So I was playing with the odds."

Oscar was impressed. As the club's official lore master, he knew that the Rabbit's Guardian Angel, almost certainly a deceased World Champion, was telekinetic, manipulating material objects like chocolate almond biscuits to induce R.R. to play the right cards. Now it appeared that he was also telepathic, exerting his benign influence on his protégé's thought processes.

If so, the notion of the Millennium venture could well be divinely inspired.

---

[1] The deal, by Pietro Bernasconi, was described by Victor Mollo in a letter to *Bridge World* as a Rabbit hand.

Chapter 2

A Three-Way Finesse

The eccentric members of the Griffins – in other words, all of them – viewed the Millennium prizes with mixed feelings. The outlandish categories excited their taste for the bizarre, but the favourites were so priced that to back them seemed futile, and to bet against them, reckless.

"I see that Papa is tipped to produce the Most Gallant Failure," remarked the Owl, as he watched the remains of his *Chateau Lafite* disappear down the Hideous Hog's capacious gullet. "Ten to one on."

Having shattered his own record time for demolishing a Chateaubriand steak for two, the Hog was in a mellow mood as he waited for his main course. "Very generous of Ladbrokes, if you ask me," he grunted. "That Greek is so cunning that he fools even himself. Have I said that before?"

"Frequently!" cried the Owl and the Corgi in unison, while even the self-effacing Toucan moved his head in what may have been the beginning of a faint nod. His bosom friend, the Rabbit, dreaming in a delicious haze of cherry brandy fumes, opened his mouth, but was too late to interrupt the Hog's infrangible flow.

"I know exactly what you were going to say, R.R., and I fully endorse your conclusions," approved H.H. "The fact that I am unquoted for that category is Ladbrokes' acceptance that failure and I are perfect strangers."

Colin the Corgi slid his glass with studied carelessness in the Hog's direction. H.H.'s predatory pounce was followed by a snarl as he realised that it was empty, and that was enough for C.C. to seize the conversational initiative. "Nonsense, H.H.," he chided. "They simply recognise your ability to manufacture a flawed masterpiece after backing yourself to win a fortune."

"Slander!" roared H.H. "I couldn't butcher a contract like that Greek if my life depended on it. It would be like Fred

Astaire treading on Ginger Rogers' toes or Rembrandt painting a moustache on his Mona Lisa. I shall content myself with the so called minor prizes, for such trivial qualities as fine card play. And this could well be the hand that will clinch one."

He seized the Rabbit's ancient copy of Nostradamus' *Prophecies* and began to scribble two hands on the title page.

"Don't worry about your book," he chortled, silencing the inevitable protest, while deftly exchanging his empty glass for the Rabbit's full one. "When I append my signature to the deal, it will double in value."

Game All. Dealer South.

R.R.
- ♠ KJ2
- ♡ J7654
- ◊ J
- ♣ K954

Papa   *W.W.*

```
    N
  W   E
    S
```

H.H.
- ♠ 63
- ♡ AKQ109
- ◊ AK10
- ♣ A103

West	North	East	South
			1♡
Pass	4♡	Pass	4♠
Pass	5♣	Pass	6♡
All Pass			

"As you all know to your cost," pontificated H.H. "I almost never misguess a two-way finesse."

"But surely ..." began the Owl, who should have known better.

"Yes, even I am not perfect in this respect, Oscar," confessed

H.H. "Do you not remember the time I lost to the Rabbit's heart queen? Charlie was his partner and he raised no objection, even though he held the card himself. Of course, R.R. had acquired his queen from another pack, but by the time it came to light, we had started the next rubber. Naturally, I blamed myself. Anyway, see if your guessing is as good as mine."

The Rabbit stared at the diagram. "I remember that hand!" he exclaimed, to everyone's amazement, including his own. "I was your partner."

"You usually are," sighed the Hog. "I am beginning to suspect that either the Gods are handicapping me, or that your invisible friend manipulates the cut."

"He should have manipulated that bidding," complained the Corgi. "It's an offence against nature."

"You are doubtless referring to R.R.'s bid of five clubs. A trifle gung-ho, I agree," nodded H.H. with massive tolerance. "But, with the final contract predestined to arrive in safe hands, quite understandable."

"I mean your puerile psychic cue bid," retorted C.C. "It might have fooled that mentally-challenged Walrus, but not Papa."

"True," agreed the Hog. "With Papa on my left, five diamonds would have been the routine psyche, but one shouldn't overdo these deceptive bids. Anyway, holding the spade ace, Themistocles would underlead it whatever I bid." He pointed sadistically towards the Owl. "Papa led the ten of spades. Your move, Oscar."

O.O. took a reflective sip of his replenished glass, held firmly in his left hand. This was poor table manners, but fine strategy: the Hog was on his right. Now the Owl was ready to perform the main duty of the Senior Kibitzer, leading the post-mortem, or, as the corpse was not yet dead, a Pre-mortem. He must be sound, but not brilliant, a Watson, but not a Holmes.

"I agree that Papa would be honour-bound to show his contempt for your spade cue bid by underleading his ace," he began. "But half the time he won't have the ace, so he is equally likely to have led from the queen."

He paused to allow the observation to sink in – it wasn't very profound, but the Rabbit and the Toucan were present.

"Time's up, Oscar," challenged the Hog, scraping a small

quantity of bread onto a huge orb of butter.

Oscar peered round the table, seeking assistance, and finding none. "The king," he declared finally. "If the knave were to lose to Walter's queen, Papa's glee when he made his ace would be insufferable."

"But what if Walter has the ace and Papa the queen?" taunted H.H.

"Then at least I won't have been caught out by a cunning underlead," rejoined O.O. "Anyway, it's a poor slam. Even if declarer guesses correctly, he will still need the diamond finesse to dispose of his club losers."

"Well spotted, Oscar," said the Hog. "And that being the case, have any of you considered a third option?" He peered round the table, seeking signs of intelligent life, and finding none. He completed the devastation of the title page by adding the East and West hands, deftly avoiding the decorative butter stains.

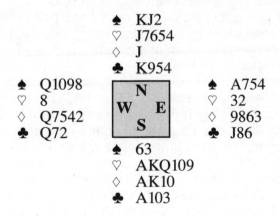

```
                    ♠ KJ2
                    ♡ J7654
                    ◇ J
                    ♣ K954
    ♠ Q1098        ┌─────────┐        ♠ A754
    ♡ 8            │    N    │        ♡ 32
    ◇ Q7542        │  W   E  │        ◇ 9863
    ♣ Q72          │    S    │        ♣ J86
                    └─────────┘
                    ♠ 63
                    ♡ AKQ109
                    ◇ AK10
                    ♣ A103
```

"The moment R.R. put down his spade suit, I called for the deuce," continued H.H. "Now put yourself in the place of the Walrus, if the concept is not too alien. I was marked with the queen by my play, and a singleton by my bidding. So he proudly tabled his ace, trusting Papa to produce the setting trick elsewhere. Mind you, I exonerate Walter of all blame. Though his expression when I guaranteed my twelfth trick by finessing the knave of spades was worthy of Greek tragedy, perhaps even of Diogenes."

"Wasn't he the one who lived in a tub?" T.T. murmured timidly to the Rabbit.

"Of course!" thundered the Hog. "Which is probably why he never wrote comedies."

"Excuse me," said the Rabbit. "But ..." Expecting to be interrupted, he paused deferentially, but the Hog, his mouth full of thinly breaded butter, smiled indulgently.

"You see," proceeded R.R. "I was thinking, er, that is to say, well, Papa can be a tricky player. He has even false-carded against me with a singleton. What if he was bluffing you, H.H.? He might have held the ace and the queen of spades, I mean ..."

"Remarkable," gasped O.O., referring both to the idea and the fact that the Rabbit, of all people, had had it.

"The ultimate double-cross," observed the equally astounded Corgi, secretly furious that he hadn't thought of it.

"It would be like playing against myself!" guffawed the Hog. But the hollow ring of his laughter suggested that he had never considered such a diabolical defence. H.H. prided himself on his capacity for self-criticism; on one occasion fifteen years ago he had miscounted his overtricks, and freely admitted it. But to have the Rabbit outshine him in a post-mortem would herald the end of civilisation as he knew it.

Then, borne by two perspiring waiters, his rack of lamb arrived, and with it inspiration. "However," he announced, "I had considered the possibility and dismissed it. Apt as he is to flashes of textbook cunning, Papa is quite incapable of original thought. Playing against a fellow master, I might have called for the knave."

"The trouble with you, R.R.," he added, rounding on the Rabbit, "is that you consistently overrate Themistocles. Why, sometimes I suspect that you actually consider him in your class."

Chapter 3

The Walrus Loses on Points

"Excellent," was the Hog's verdict, as he placed his pristine pudding spoon onto an equally clean plate.

The rack of lamb was a distant memory as he savoured the aftertaste of his *crêpes Suzette*. They had been laced with two glasses of Grand Marnier, and precisely the right measure of Armagnac – half a bottle.

He carved a modest slice of Stilton and had it passed round the table while he addressed himself to the remaining kilogram. In front of him was a schooner of Taylors' 70 and several others were within clutching distance.

The Toucan had a firm hold on his balloon glass of antique Hine, but his vigilance would not last forever, and when it faltered, the Hog would be ready.

Glowing with goodwill towards his fellow diners, he decided to direct his powers of vilification at absent Griffins. As it was almost ten minutes since he had vilified the Walrus, that seemed a good place to start.

"I believe that an antique abacus is to be awarded for pointless point-counting," he observed. "If so, Walter should claim it with this deal."

He astonished the company by producing four hands, neatly inscribed on a six-by-four card. "I may include this quaint little miniature in my memoirs," he explained, as he passed it round, anti-portwise.

East/West Game. Dealer South.

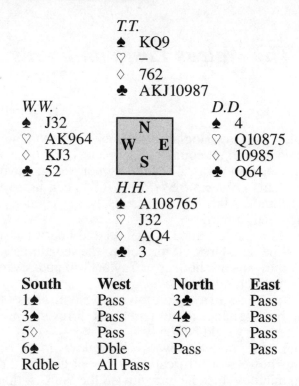

T.T.
- ♠ KQ9
- ♡ –
- ◇ 762
- ♣ AKJ10987

W.W.
- ♠ J32
- ♡ AK964
- ◇ KJ3
- ♣ 52

D.D.
- ♠ 4
- ♡ Q10875
- ◇ 10985
- ♣ Q64

H.H.
- ♠ A108765
- ♡ J32
- ◇ AQ4
- ♣ 3

South	West	North	East
1♠	Pass	3♣	Pass
3♠	Pass	4♠	Pass
5◇	Pass	5♡	Pass
6♠	Dble	Pass	Pass
Rdble	All Pass		

"You were my partner, T.T.," H.H. reminded the Toucan. "I forgave you for not bidding the slam, and did your job for you. Walter doubled in outrage that we had at most twenty-eight points. My redouble was entirely selfless; it added only a hundred pounds or so to my winnings. I wanted to teach W.W. a valuable lesson: to deduct three points for his defensive skill and a further six for my dummy play. How he could double on a miserable three count I do not know, but I suppose basic Acol remains a mystery to him. Anyway, he led his heart king, asking for count. I'm sure that you will all agree that declarer's winning line doesn't exactly leap to mind."

His assertion was greeted by a curl of the lip from the Corgi, a snore from the Rabbit and a vigorous nod from the Toucan, who, however many hands were exposed, found even two-card endings a struggle.

O.O. said nothing. According to one of his Rhodes scholars, this is what had occurred:

After ruffing the lead in dummy, H.H. cashed the ♣AK, discarding a heart, and continued with the ♣J, ruffing flamboyantly with the ace.

As Dolly, with a soft coo of regret, played her ♣Q, Walter choked with indignation. A slam on only twenty-four points!

Though he had retired on the day he qualified, the Walrus was a well-known accountant, who found point-counting and signalling the most thrilling adventures since the invention of double-entry bookkeeping. Bidding slams without the regulation quota was a fiscal monstrosity that cried out for punishment. He frantically searched his hand for a trump higher than the ace. Finding none, he threw the ♡9, to remind everyone, including himself, that he still held the ace.

"Well done, Walter," admired the Hog. "You know more about signalling than Samuel Morse. Or even Fred Semaphore," he added for good measure. He crossed to dummy's ♠K, and advanced the ♣10, pitching his last heart. When Walter ruffed, this was the position:

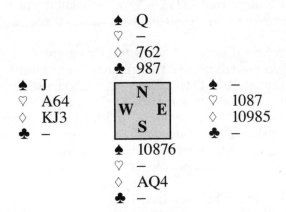

At this point, Walter had an uncanny premonition that crime was about to pay. The subtle clues were the three master clubs on the green baize, and the smirk on the Hog's pink face. W.W. tried the ♡A, but it was ruffed in hand, and the ♠Q provided the entry to dummy's winners.

"You had twenty-four points!" bellowed the Walrus.

"I know," the Hog apologised. "Usually I make do with less. Luckily, adversity has honed my skills to heights undreamed of. I take no credit for this. As Milton remarked – or it may have been me – 'Greatness has been thrust upon me!'"

Having concluded his own self-satisfied version of events, the Hog described how Walter's vast bulk had quaked with disapproval. It was received wisdom at the Griffins that when the Walrus visited his tailor to try on some new smoking jackets, the only thing that fitted him was the cubicle.

"As I recall, Timothy," H.H. leered benignly at the Toucan, "thanks to Walter's bidding and my card play, we won a rubber of twenty-five, which I am sure is why you invited us to this splendid feast. No, don't protest – you thoroughly deserve the honour."

A Record for Walter

"What a pity we cannot honour the Worst Player of the Millennium," regretted O.O., a few days later. "In the Rabbit, the Toucan and the Walrus, we have three outstanding contenders."

"With respect, Oscar ..." ventured Peregrine Penguin.

"I wish you wouldn't use that phrase," said Oscar testily. "It invariably implies that I am talking utter nonsense, and that you are about to employ your superior intellect to refute it."

P.P. considered this at length. "'With respect' is shorter," he concluded. "But, I'm afraid, your claim has two flaws. First, although R.R. has his moments, because of his unbridled luck he lacks the consistency one would expect from a candidate for low office."

"*With respect*, P.P.," retaliated the Owl, "no man of taste would deny the greatness of *King Lear* or *Macbeth*, because of the crude excesses of *Titus Andronicus*. And if we forgive Shakespeare's off days, shouldn't we turn a blind eye to the Rabbit's on days? He should be judged at the peak of his disability." He poured two glasses of postprandial port. "But you spoke of two flaws."

"Some years ago," recalled Peregrine, "we loaned Walter to you while our club was being redecorated – his allergies, you know. That nobody has seen fit to tell him that the paint is now dry doesn't alter the fact that he is still a Unicorn."

"A technicality, but a valid one," conceded Oscar. "But let's agree that the Rabbit is disqualified for inconsistency and the final choice is between our T.T. and your W.W."

"For our Walrus," boasted P.P., "brain surgery would be a minor operation."

"For our Toucan," countered Oscar proudly, "decapitation would not be an intellectual threat. And no one can butcher a contract like Timothy."

"But, *with the greatest respect*," argued P.P., "if H.H. is the ultimate contract hog, T.T. is the champion dummy hog. Having no delusions of adequacy, he confines his blunders largely to defence. And no one can butcher an auction like Walter. He is the complete all-rounder, our abominable Crichton. Let me show you an example of vintage Walrus from his mid-Unicorn period. His partner was Colin the Corgi, newly arrived from Oxbridge with the ink still dry on his fourth class honours degree in Manchurian Theosophy. It was not until he joined the Griffins that he upgraded it to a starred first."

He neatly sketched this innocent looking diagram:

East/West Game. Dealer North.

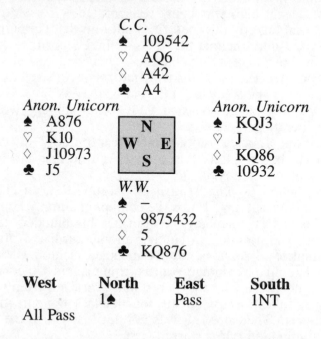

C.C.
♠ 109542
♡ AQ6
◇ A42
♣ A4

Anon. Unicorn
♠ A876
♡ K10
◇ J10973
♣ J5

Anon. Unicorn
♠ KQJ3
♡ J
◇ KQ86
♣ 10932

W.W.
♠ –
♡ 9875432
◇ 5
♣ KQ876

West	North	East	South
	1♠	Pass	1NT
All Pass			

"Try to imagine the torrents of anguish cascading through Walter's mind, assuming he has one," recommended P.P. "Every fibre of his being screamed out against the fiscal blasphemy of responding with only five and a quarter points. Torquemada could not have devised a more exquisite torture."

"Probably not," confirmed Oscar. "Though the executioners of the later Ming dynasty might have come close."

"Amateurs," scoffed the Penguin with a dismissive flap. "Yet some uncanny instinct – I hesitate to call it judgment – told Walter Walrus that by passing he would be missing the chance of a part score. Two hearts was an unthinkable travesty, so in a voice quivering with torment, he responded a courageous one no trump."

"Did the earth shake?" enquired O.O.

"No, but his chair collapsed," replied Peregrine. "And when a replacement was found everyone passed, and West, whose name I'm afraid he'd forgotten, led the jack of diamonds. W.W. took the first trick and cashed three rounds of clubs. When the suit didn't break, he tried the heart finesse. I will leave you to guess his comment when it succeeded, and he gathered in an easy eleven tricks."

"Would 'I had only five and a quarter, partner' fit the bill?" speculated the Owl.

"Word perfect," approved the Penguin. "And the Corgi's rejoinder was equally predictable. 'Congratulations, Walter.' he jeered. 'Let it never again be said that you are a slave to the Milton Work point count. A less flexible player might have scored minus fifty or so by passing my one spade bid. How anyone could consider a heart contract, in which we would make thirteen tricks by normal play, is a complete mystery. After all, you had only seven of them'."

"Your members must miss Colin," smiled Oscar.

"Oh, but they still see him from time to time," said Peregrine. "You can always tell when he drops in, by the frantic rush to the backgammon tables."

Chapter 4

Sophia the Siren

When Themistocles Papadopoulos saw the unflattering odds against his taking a Brilliancy Prize, the enraged ship-owner mortgaged a medium-sized tanker to place a bet so colossal that he supplanted the Hog as the bookies' favourite. Now, having forsaken his Hugo Boss smoking jacket for a T-shirt quoting his new odds, Papa was high man on the Griffins totem pole.

Until he went too far ...

For such an exhibitionist to bring his personal kibitzer to the club was not without precedent, but the advent of the voluptuous Sophia was a threat to the very fabric of the Griffins' snug society.

"She spells trouble," warned an ancient Griffin, who had left his life-support machine to witness at first hand the phenomenon of Sophia the Siren.

She was introduced as Papa's distant cousin, but her beauty and charm suggested that the distance was astronomical. Compliments flowed from her full magenta lips. She praised Papa's sportsmanship, Charlie the Chimp's integrity, and the frequency with which the Toucan played from the correct hand. She greeted the Corgi's adolescent wit with ripples of melodic laughter, and Karapet's hard luck stories with moist eyes. In Sophia's presence, feuds floundered, enmity evaporated, and the savage cut and thrust for which the club was renowned was supplanted by the occasional pusillanimous prod.

"I'm afraid there's nothing in the rules against it," Oscar told the deputation hastily formed to demand the restoration of the old order.

"There ought to be a rule against those legs," growled the Walrus. Having counted them (she had two) and added three points for length, he decided they had no further place in the philosophy of an unmarried bachelor. "What's the point of all this legislation on sex discrimination if we refuse to discriminate?" he grumbled. "If we're not careful, we'll have a monstrous regiment beating at our doors."

"Thank you, Walter," said Oscar. "We'll bear your warning in mind."

Some years ago, the committee had flouted tradition by admitting two female members. But Dolly the Dove was so modest that nobody had so much as glimpsed her lower limbs, while Molly the Mule's solid underpinning was designed solely to propel her between tables. Sophia's legs were sculpted to double the blood pressure of hardened misogynists, and triple the number of revokes.

Only the Hog was immune. No display of pulchritude could diminish his effortless skills, and her effect on his opponents raised his winnings to obscene levels.

"We must keep up with the times," he proclaimed. "Some of us," he added, looking round accusingly, "have become far too preoccupied with bridge, and food and drink. That is why I have given up boiled spinach, Venezuelan Burgundy and overcalls on three-card suits. The new Millennium is our opportunity to focus on higher-ranking things. Papa's cousin is the cultural equivalent of a McKenney signal."

The insipid nature of the Griffin's disputes prevailed until, sitting between Papa and the Rueful Rabbit, Sophia witnessed the following deal:

Love All. Dealer East.

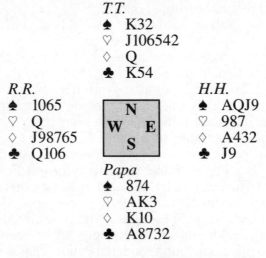

T.T.
♠ K32
♡ J106542
◇ Q
♣ K54

R.R.
♠ 1065
♡ Q
◇ J98765
♣ Q106

H.H.
♠ AQJ9
♡ 987
◇ A432
♣ J9

Papa
♠ 874
♡ AK3
◇ K10
♣ A8732

West	North	East	South
		1NT	Dble
2◇	3◇!	Pass	3♡!
Pass	4♡	All Pass	

Timothy's three diamonds was a polite request for Papa to play the contract, which was about as necessary as requesting a hen to cluck when she laid an egg.

Against four hearts, R.R., probably hoping for a ruff, led his singleton trump queen. After a cursory glance at dummy, Papa gave his cousin a patronising wink.

"Not a hand to overtax the intellect," he said. "But you may find it instructive. Observe." Taking the queen with his king, he advanced the ◇10. His plan was faultless: when the Hog captured with his ace, the stage would be set to park one of dummy's clubs on the ◇Q. Then a ruff would establish the suit for two spade discards.

"I don't know who your cousin expects to instruct you." The Hog rotated his thick pink neck to leer seductively at Sophia. "But I suppose it's me," he concluded, and promptly ducked!

With a gnash of expensive dentistry, Papa considered the effect of this deadly and inconsiderate defence. He would now have to lose a club to the Hog, but how? Hopefully he placed an innocent ♣2 on the table. The Rabbit, to whom playing second hand high was almost second nature, smoothly inserted the ten. Papa ducked, hoping, with good reason, that R.R. would do the wrong thing.

The Rabbit's sensitive nose twitched nervously as he inspected H.H.'s club nine. He knew a McWhatsit signal when he saw one, but he couldn't remember whether it called for a return of the higher ranking suit, or the highest-ranking card of that suit. When he eventually concluded that the ♠10 met both conditions, he duly produced it, dashing Papa's last hope.

"Bravo!" cried S.S., clapping her hands with joy, and turning her gorgeous head towards the startled Rabbit. "It was your lead of the singleton trump which made the brilliancy possible, and your miraculous choice of the ♠10 was the *coup de grâce*. You must be the gentleman my cousin refers to as the second best player in the club."

R.R. had been paid the ultimate compliment: he had been mistaken for someone else. As a roseate glow suffused his entire body, Sophia flashed her perfect teeth at the Hog. "And it follows that you, Sir, with your incredible duck at trick two, must be the bes..."

"Next deal!" bellowed Papa, just in time to cut off his cousin's four-letter word, but not to stifle the ill-bred guffaw of his archenemy.

"Normally I would leave it to your illustrious relative to explain the finer points of my defence," H.H. twisted the knife. "But as he is about to deal, that duty must fall on my humble shoulders. The trump lead revealed that declarer held three of them. To justify his take-out double, he would need a good club suit, but I had to assume he was missing the queen, or four hearts would have been laydown, the type of contract with which Themistocles has built his world-wide reputation. Furthermore, he would ..."

"No bid!" screamed Papa, after the merest glance at his cards, while players and kibitzers beamed with relief.

Disharmony had returned to the Griffins.

Chapter 5

The Witch of Ararat

"I didn't know that Karapet was a betting man," remarked an anonymous Griffin to the inhabitants of an empty bar.

Karapet Djoulikyan, the Free Armenian, incensed at being a mere 33/1 on to scoop the Unluckiest Play Trophy, had wagered three months bridge losses to ensure that the odds soared to a more realistic three figures. In 1423, the Wicked Witch of Ararat had cast a spell, guaranteeing that, when a Djoulikyan was at the helm, either the adverse trumps would break eight-nil, or the contract would be set by a diabolical mis-defence.

The present heir to the family misfortune had the melancholy eyes and long, lugubrious nose of a man inured to life's vicissitudes. But the set of that lean Djoulikyan jaw-line proclaimed that he had resolved not just to accept a lifetime of disaster, but to revel in it. Karapet was the ultimate genetic triumph of twenty generations of unshakeable pessimists.

Twelve of the first twenty-nine hands he submitted for the trophy (a cracked Georgian mirror) involved the Rueful Rabbit. Two of R.R.'s inspired defences were due to his inability to sort his cards. This was by no means his fault. He had offered to provide the club with special packs, containing royal blue spades and pea green hearts, but the Hog had pooh-poohed the idea.

"It isn't the expense I'm concerned about," H.H. assured the Rabbit. "I realise that any man who cuts me as his partner nine times out of ten can well afford it. But mis-sorting is the best part of your game, the very cornerstone of your genius."

"But …" objected the Rabbit.

"Exactly," agreed the Hog. "And very well put. But has it occurred to you that with your cards in correct order you will be forced to depend solely on brain power?"

Seeing the look of panic on his friend's face, he produced his clinching argument. "Besides, with pea green hearts, you will be

depriving the public of your celebrated hold-up plays."
   The hand H.H. referred to inevitably saw the Rabbit opposing
Karapet:

East/West Game. Dealer South.

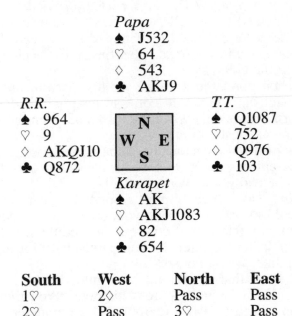

Papa
♠ J532
♡ 64
◇ 543
♣ AKJ9

R.R.
♠ 964
♡ 9
◇ AKQJ10
♣ Q872

T.T.
♠ Q1087
♡ 752
◇ Q976
♣ 103

Karapet
♠ AK
♡ AKJ1083
◇ 82
♣ 654

South	West	North	East
1♡	2◇	Pass	Pass
2♡	Pass	3♡	Pass
4♡	All Pass		

   Regular students of the Griffins will realise that R.R.'s
vulnerable overcall was based on his mistaking his heart queen
for the ◇Q.
   The Rabbit anguished over his lead against four hearts. At his
left sat Sophia the Siren, who had dubbed him the second best
player in the club, and he would hate to slither down her ranking
list. A top diamond stood out a mile, but which? What was that
mnemonic the Walrus had taught him? Ah yes: 'A for Attitude,
K for Count.' Striving to appear learned, he selected the ace and
continued with the king.
   He even noticed that Timothy had echoed with the nine and
six. Such an obvious attitude signal could mean only one thing:
for some reason, his best friend wanted to ruff the third round.

With a coy peek at Sophia, R.R. produced the ◊J, hoping that she, if not Timothy, would recognise it as a McCarthy signal, demanding a spade return. Not that R.R. held anything in spades, but it might have confused Karapet.

To R.R.'s surprise, his partner followed low. Had his signal been a cunning psyche? Declarer ruffed, crossed to dummy's ♣A, and finessed the ♡J. When R.R.'s ♡9 appeared, Karapet frowned. He never expected his finesses to succeed. But as he never expected trumps to break, he returned to the table with the ♣K and repeated the finesse.

The Rabbit pondered sagely over his discard, and decided that his imaginary ◊Q would confirm his putative desire for a spade return. It was only when the card landed on the table that it turned miraculously into the ♡Q!

Bowing his head in shame, he gathered the trick, and set the contract by cashing the ♣Q. Now his delectable admirer would see him as he really was, warts and all.

His heart leapt when Sophia rapped the table ecstatically. "Magnifico!" she cried. "Baring your trump queen required not only genius, my friend, but courage. You could see that every card was right for declarer, so you persuaded him to take the only losing line. Was it not so?"

"Well I, er … that is, I thought …" gulped R.R.

Papa could no longer suppress his rage. "You thought that your queen of hearts was a diamond!" he thundered. "And so you fluked a masterpiece I created years ago."

He sneered at the gaping kibitzers. "It is said that, given enough time, a monkey seated at a word processor will eventually produce the entire works of Shakespeare. I suppose we can look forward to R.R. reproducing all my brilliancies."

"He already has," quipped the Corgi. "Both of them."

"Do not blame R.R., partner," Karapet advised the fuming Greek. "It was the luck of the Djoulikyans." He leaned mournfully towards Sophia. "Did I ever tell you what the Witch of Ararat did in 1423?"

S.S. turned to him, her eyes shining. "You did," she said. "But please tell me again."

As Karapet launched into his saga, Papa and the Toucan quietly joined the kibitzers as they crossed the room to watch the riveting spectacle of Dolly the Dove playing Solitaire, while the unfortunate Rabbit dealt the next hand.

Karapet in Luck

"Did you hear what R.R. did to me on Thursday?" asked Karapet, interposing his body between Oscar and the only avenue of escape.

"As a matter of fact, Colin told me about it," lied the Owl, desperately looking for a gap in the Armenian's defence. Seeing none, he sank helplessly into the nearest chair, to consider the feasibility of a late career change.

Karapet was again the victim of inspired mis-sorting.

The Rabbit had been suffering a bad run. Playing in three no trumps with eleven top tricks, he had only managed eight of them. Then he had botched a grand slam by spurning a winning finesse in favour of a losing endplay.

Misfortunes always come in threes, and now he was partnered by Charlie the Chimp, the Black Sheep of the Griffins. Charlie was notorious for (amongst other failings) his keen interest in every hand except the one he was playing.

"Why did you double the Blackwood response in that last rubber?" he enquired, as the Rabbit picked up his hand.

"It was lead-directing," R.R. explained proudly. "Asking for a club lead."

"But our opponents had agreed spades," persisted Charlie. "You would have been on lead."

"Would I?" responded R.R. "Oh yes, I, er ... I wanted to remind myself to lead a club."

"But you led a diamond."

"Did I?" The Rabbit appeared bemused. "Then it just goes to show that you can't always trust these fancy conventions. Your partner may not understand them. I remember the time when I was playing with Timothy and we both made a splinter bid in the same suit; and he passed my S.O.S. redouble. I don't know if you've ever played in a nil-nil fit, Charlie, but it makes trump control very difficult, and ..."

"One heart!" barked Karapet.

Love All. Dealer South.

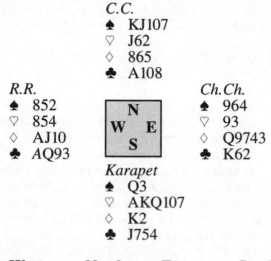

C.C.
♠ KJ107
♡ J62
◇ 865
♣ A108

R.R.
♠ 852
♡ 854
◇ AJ10
♣ AQ93

Ch.Ch.
♠ 964
♡ 93
◇ Q9743
♣ K62

Karapet
♠ Q3
♡ AKQ107
◇ K2
♣ J754

West	North	East	South
			1♡
Pass	2♡	Pass	3♣
Pass	4♡	All Pass	

Devoted Griffins followers will guess from the diagram that the distracted Rabbit had stuffed his spade ace amongst his clubs, but his inspired lead against Karapet's four hearts may require explanation.

On his birthday, R.R.'s maiden niece had given him a copy of *Fifty Bridge Tips for Beginners*. Browsing through it out of politeness, he discovered that forty-eight of them were new to him. Now, concealed cunningly in the dust jacket of *Bridge in the Ninth Dimension*, the volume had become his constant companion.

His favourite nugget was, 'When in Doubt, Lead a Trump'. To one who was invariably in doubt, this was manna from heaven. It was with Hog-like confidence that he led the ♡4.

Karapet played a second trump and registered only mild surprise when everyone followed. He drew the last trump before playing on spades. The queen of spades held, and a second spade to dummy's king was also allowed to win. Glowering when the ace failed to appear, he played a diamond to his ◊K, and gave a sigh of resignation when it was headed by R.R.'s ace.

Suddenly the Rabbit noticed that the pack contained two club aces. When he realised that the error was his and not Waddingtons', his face assumed every colour from pink to vermilion. He was about to play what he now knew to be the ♠A, when his legendary sixth sense told him to persist with diamonds, and sink the contract.

"A masterly defence R.R.," grinned the perceptive Corgi. "Aren't you lucky the Hog talked you out of ordering royal blue spades?"

"His luck had nothing to do with it," lamented Karapet. "It was my curse which caused him to misplay so cleverly." His elongated face looked more lugubrious than ever, and his audience gave a collective shudder. They knew that a Chekhovian dirge was on its way, but there was nowhere to hide.

"If I had a swimming pool it would catch fire," he informed them. "If I took an aspirin it would give me a headache. And the day my ship comes in," he added with a tragic shrug, "there will be a dock strike."

"And if you had a twin brother, he would forget your birthday," added C.C., with a considerate air of melancholy.

When Karapet submitted the deal to the Hog, who advised the committee for the Unluckiest Play competition, H.H. gave the Armenian's shoulder a sympathetic squeeze. "My dear friend," he chortled. "I believe you have given me this by mistake. Surely it qualifies for Luckiest Deal category."

Had a gauntlet been handy, Karapet would have hurled it at the Hog's feet. "Lucky!" he croaked.

"But of course," asserted H.H. "You were lucky that you held that precious spade honour. Leading the second round to your queen ensures that, if the defence refuses the trick, you are in a position to finesse the eight of clubs safely. You would lose two diamonds, one club, and no heart."

Showing remarkable courage, the Armenian stared at his diagram and saw that the Hog was right, but that was no excuse for such a scurrilous accusation.

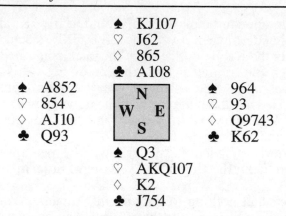

♠ KJ107
♡ J62
◊ 865
♣ A108

♠ A852
♡ 854
◊ AJ10
♣ Q93

♠ 964
♡ 93
◊ Q9743
♣ K62

♠ Q3
♡ AKQ107
◊ K2
♣ J754

"I only wish I had your luck," H.H. teased his helplessly fulminating victim. "I understand you owe it all to that benevolent spell cast by the Good Fairy of Ararat in 1066. When you have a spare moment, you might let me have her name and address."

Karapet is expected to present his letter of resignation as soon as his secretary has corrected the typographical errors on page 29.

Chapter 6

An Ideal Husband

"I have fond memories of Timothy Toucan's first appearance at the Griffins," reminisced the Owl. "I forget the exact date, but I believe it was the year that his age overtook his I.Q. An empty limousine drew up outside the club, and Timothy got out."

"He must have been a welcome sight," remarked Peregrine Penguin, Oscar's opposite number at the Unicorns.

"Indeed," said Oscar. "He was obviously a man of means, but every inch a born loser. Modest, deferential to his betters, which meant everyone except the Walrus, he was embraced by all, especially the Rabbit, who no longer regarded himself as the Worst Player in the Western Hemisphere."

"The meek have yet to inherit the earth," nodded Peregrine. "But T.T. is the heir apparent. We would love to have him at the Unicorns, though I'm afraid that we could never afford the transfer fee." He gave a doleful sigh. "That long rubicund nose would look well in our Regency dining room, and our house Burgundy would nurture it splendidly. Is the dear fellow in the running for any of your millennium prizes?"

"Alas, no," replied the Owl. "We considered a trophy for Humility, but he would be too humble to accept it." He sipped his Madeira reflectively. "I heard from a reliable source that when Timothy started to write his autobiography, he reached chapter six before he noticed he wasn't in it."

Peregrine leaned back, puffing out his chest as he savoured his *Remy Martin*. His black sleeves, contrasting with the broad expanse of white shirt, heightened the bird-like appearance to which he owed his nickname.

"The Toucan should provide the ideal partner for Molly the Mule," he conjectured. "His highly developed sense of guilt compels him to take the blame for everything, while Molly, your rampant feminist, must always be in the right. And since that requires someone to be always in the wrong, they would enjoy a true symbiosis."

Oscar was impressed. P.P.'s shrewd analysis showed why he was regarded as the second best kibitzer in London.

"Tell me, Oscar," continued the Penguin. "How did Molly react to your proposed award for the Best Play by a Lady?"

"Predictably." O.O. grimaced at the memory. "In protest against its sexist nature, she chained herself to the railings outside the club. It took the committee two days to cancel the category, and a further three to arrange for her release."

He put down his Madeira with a carefree abandon which indicated that the Hog was nowhere to be seen, and produced his Morocco-bound kibitzer's notebook.

"To prove your point, here is a fine example of the Mule and the Toucan in harness. Wonderful spectator sport, and it will certainly win her the prize for Persistence in the Post-mortem, which I believe is a wood etching of Robert the Bruce's spider."

Love All. Dealer West. Both sides 60 towards.

Anonymous Griffin
♠ 2
♡ J432
◇ A1098765
♣ 2

T.T.
♠ Q108753
♡ Q109
◇ KJ
♣ Q5

M.M.
♠ —
♡ A765
◇ Q43
♣ KJ7643

H.H.
♠ AKJ964
♡ K8
◇ 2
♣ A1098

South	West	North	East
	Pass	Pass	1♣
2♠	Dble	Pass	3♣
Dble	Pass	3◇	Pass
3♠	Dble	All Pass	

As usual when both sides had part-scores, the auction was somewhat Neanderthal. The Toucan bounced nervously in his seat before settling on the ♡10 as his opening lead. Shaking her head in disbelief, Molly won with the ace and returned the suit. With a grunt of pleasure, the Hog seized the trick, cashed the ♣A, and trumped a club.

After H.H. had ruffed a heart, crossed to the ♢A and ruffed a diamond, T.T.'s only assets were six spades, which turned mysteriously into liabilities. When the Hog exited with a club, Timothy had to ruff and lead a trump. Declarer won, played his last club, and, gloating charmingly, claimed an overtrick.

"Why did you double them into game?" demanded Molly.

"I'm sorry," apologised the Toucan. "I'm afraid I'm right off form today. I thought that with their part-score of sixty, they were already in a game contract."

"Typical male excuse," scoffed the unsinkable M.M. "And why didn't you lead my suit?"

"I see now that I should have done. It was very remiss of me. Er, remind me ... what was your suit?"

"Clubs!" shrilled Molly. "And a trump lead might have been even better."

"I believe you," commiserated the Toucan. "I let you down badly; I was a fool even to consider leading your suit. And I confess that, despite your opening bid, I should never have doubled on only ten points and a six-card trump suit. But I was following the Law of Total Tricks, you know."

"Of course I know," retorted the Mule. "There's a total of thirteen tricks. And they made ten of them."

"I know, and I'm terribly ..."

"It's your deal," sniffed Molly. "Do you think you can manage it by yourself, or do you want me to do it for you?"

When Oscar had finished his account, the Penguin gave a knowing nod. "Poor Timothy," he said. "If there was no Molly the Mule, he would have to invent one."

"Well observed, P.P.," said the Owl. "But in her own way, Molly was being kind. When a masochist begs to be chastised, only a sadist would be cruel enough to refuse him."

Peregrine gazed at his friend in admiration. Oscar had shown why he was considered London's second best kibitzer.

Chapter 7

The Distinguished Bridge Author

"It will all end in tears," predicted Oscar, to the world at large. None of its inhabitants dared to contradict him.

The gentle Rabbit and the humble Toucan, the two most sought after opponents in the Western Hemisphere (the Walrus was away on holiday in Vladivostok) were up against it. On R.R.'s left lurked the Secretary Bird, poised to pounce on the minutest infringement. On his right was a Distinguished Bridge Author.

Although he had written fifty-seven books, several of which had been published, the D.B.A. was an unknown quantity. He only appeared at the Griffins every five years or so, and this was his first visit. Yet during the previous rubber, his analyses were so penetrating that Oscar the Owl decided to propose him for membership ... of the Unicorns.

Abstruse conventions were forbidden at rubber bridge, but when the Rabbit and the Toucan were in harness, their opponents generously allowed them to misuse as many as they liked.

"Are we playing Acol or Precision, Timothy?" enquired the Rabbit.

"The best bits of each," enthused the Toucan, always anxious to co-operate. "Let's play it by ear."

"Roman Key Card Blackwood?"

"If you wish. But only on slam hands, if you don't mind."

"And the multi-two diamonds?" ventured R.R. hopefully.

"By all means," agreed T.T. "Would you mind going over it again?"

"Certainly," wittered the Rabbit. "It can have four different meanings, or perhaps five, but we can only use three of them. To keep it simple, I suggest we ..."

Oscar winced at the prospect of seeing his friends play in a series of one-nil trump fits. They had been thrown to the lions, and every thumb in the stadium was pointing inexorably downwards.

But O.O. had reckoned without the Rabbit's Guardian Angel. On the first deal, R.R. blundered his way into four spades, which, labouring under the delusion that he was in three no-trumps, he made with a trump squeeze.

"Well played," acknowledged the D.B.A., making a note of the hand while R.R. dealt the next. "Have you read my book on Esoteric Pseudo-Squeezes?"

"Not yet," said the ubiquitous Corgi. "He's waiting for the film version."

Ignoring him, the author resumed his conversation with his fellow expert. "I've heard about your club's Millennium competitions. A splendid idea. I hoped they might provide a piece or two for my column. Tell me, are you in the running for anything?"

"Er, I ... that is, it's a little early to ... so I don't think ..."

"He is certain to win the first prize for misdealing," rasped the Secretary Bird. "I have sixteen cards."

R.R. was visibly distressed. Next to shuffling, dealing was the best part of his game. Squaring his round shoulders, he proved it by throwing in his Yarborough and dealing himself a twenty-point hand. As he picked it up, a waiter brought him a large cherry brandy and a plate of his favourite chocolate almond biscuits.

Oscar leaned forward and rubbed his hands with renewed hope. He sensed that the Guardian Angel was pulling out all the stops.

North/South Game. Dealer South.

T.T.
♠ AJ
♡ Q1092
◇ Q32
♣ AJ86

S.B.
♠ 976542
♡ 8
◇ 10985
♣ 43

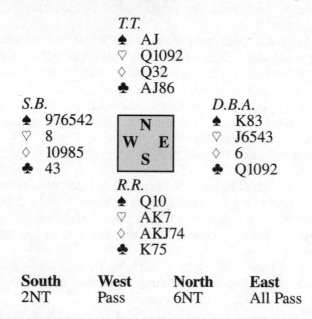

D.B.A.
♠ K83
♡ J6543
◇ 6
♣ Q1092

R.R.
♠ Q10
♡ AK7
◇ AKJ74
♣ K75

South	West	North	East
2NT	Pass	6NT	All Pass

Timothy considered seeking a heart fit, but he wasn't sure whether they were playing three clubs as Baron, Stayman, or a Mississippi Transfer. So, after carefully reviewing the entire auction to make sure he wouldn't be declarer, he leapt to six no trumps in a fearless whisper.

S.B. led the ◇10. Anxious not to destroy the impression he had made, R.R. decided on the novel tactic of planning the hand before playing from dummy. With the aid of a pencil and paper, he counted his tricks – eleven on top. If he took the three available finesses and only one of them succeeded, it would be his twelfth. Destiny decreed that he would go one down, provided he refused the third finesse, but S.B. and his Guardian Angel had other ideas.

Flushed with confidence from his fruitful flirtation with higher mathematics, R.R. won with his ◇A. He played a second diamond to the queen on which the D.B.A. threw a heart. Before he had gathered the trick, a large piece of biscuit stuck in his throat. A gulp of cherry brandy cleared the obstruction, but a violent coughing fit ensued. Searching for a handkerchief, he placed his cards on the table. It was only when he recovered that he noticed to his horror that they were face-upwards.

There was a predatory gleam in S.B.'s pince-nez. "Are you making a claim?" he asked, his voice silky with menace.

"Of course he is," stated his erudite partner. "To a player who can bring off a trump squeeze without pausing for thought, it will be blindingly obvious that the slam is frigid as soon as I discard on the second round of diamonds. He will now cash the club king, advance a second club towards the table and simply cover your card, expertly end-playing me. Whatever I lead will provide his twelfth trick."

The Toucan bounced with admiration. "Brilliantly played, partner," he gushed.

"One moment," commanded S.B., with a sinister twitch of his thin, bloodless lips. "There is no legal precedent for a defender making a statement on declarer's behalf, R.R. is required to play the hand without taking a finesse."

"Can I draw trumps?" pleaded the crestfallen Rabbit.

"Certainly. You happen to be in six no-trumps, but don't let that deter you."

"Dear, dear!" The D.B.A. gave a reproving shake of his head. "He doesn't need to finesse. Running the diamonds will put me under intolerable pressure. I must retain my guarded king of spades, so I must find three discards from hearts and clubs. Declarer now runs whichever suit I discard from. It's a textbook progressive squeeze. He makes thirteen tricks, which costs us an extra point, I believe. I make it a rubber of eighteen."

"Enough!" cried S.B., his Adam's apple throbbing with magisterial rage. "I must inform you, Sir, that you have a duty to your partner, not to declarer. The law cannot function when the victim decides to appear as a witness for the defence." He rose with dignity and strode majestically from the room, muttering under his sibilant breath.

"Charming fellow," remarked the D.B.A. "Is he a judge, by any chance? Not that I've got anything against lawyers, but ..."

"Nor have I," agreed the Corgi. "It's just that ninety-nine percent of them give the others a bad name."

A Transparent Deception

Soon afterwards, kibitzing learnedly, the D.B.A. became aware of a highly charged atmosphere. Any member could have told him that H.C.A.'s were frequent at the Griffins, and that the present one was due to the waves of hostility radiating from Papa to the Hog, from the Walrus to Molly the Mule, and from M.M. to mankind in general.

Molly was generating a particularly searing current in the direction of Sophia the Siren. It was one of S.S.'s Gucci days, and every chic detail was a red rag to the Mule's bullish feminism.

"I've read all your books," Sophia was telling the Distinguished Bridge Author. "May I bring them along for you to autograph?"

"I shouldn't," the Hog whispered to her. "The unsigned copies have a great rarity value. You were lucky to have found one."

"Bridge books are a complete waste of time," snapped Molly. "They're always telling you how to play hands that turn up once a century, if that. Whose bid is it?"

"Mine, I believe," the Hog informed her. "But I prefer to sort my hand before I bid it. It's a tip I found in a bridge book. It has improved my game tremendously."

"I didn't think that was possible," broke in Papa.

"Thank you," the Hog smiled sweetly. "I'll lend it to you, if you like. There is a chapter on 'True Carding', which you might find useful."

The author scribbled furiously. If this kept up, he would soon have enough material for two new books.

H.H. was in black mood. After three hours of play, he was only two hundred pounds up, well below his budget, and hardly enough to pay for a decent dinner, not that he was likely to pick up the bill. If things went on like this he might as well give up bridge and become a brain surgeon. But his snarl as he concluded his attack on Molly soon faded when he found himself gazing at a rock-crusher. With his favorite opponent on his right, life couldn't be sweeter.

Love All. Dealer South.

M.M.
♠ 983
♡ J762
◇ 85
♣ 10643

W.W.
♠ 72
♡ 10943
◇ QJ92
♣ AKQ

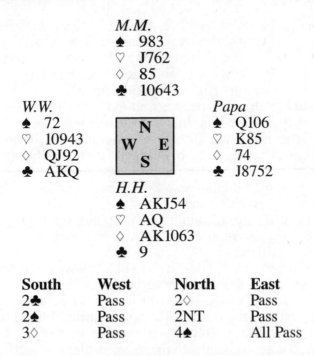

Papa
♠ Q106
♡ K85
◇ 74
♣ J8752

H.H.
♠ AKJ54
♡ AQ
◇ AK1063
♣ 9

South	West	North	East
2♣	Pass	2◇	Pass
2♠	Pass	2NT	Pass
3◇	Pass	4♠	All Pass

The Hog gave his opening bid several seconds of deep thought. As he had two good five-card suits, each biddable at the eight-level, he confidently opened two clubs. He had a bad moment when Molly paused before her four spade bid. He feared she was going to leap to five diamonds, which she had mentioned first, but his ghastly bidding error went unpunished.

Walter led the ♣Q, and Molly put down her meagre collection with a defiant thump. "It isn't much, partner, but I've got my bid," she asserted. "So stop sneering at me as if I was a perfect idiot."

"I wouldn't dream of it, Molly," purred the Hog. "Nobody's perfect."

Themistocles played the ♣8 on the opening lead, a false card that had his two essential hallmarks; it was cunning and meaningless. Walter continued with the club ace, and looked distinctly perturbed when H.H. ruffed. When the Hog took the percentage line of playing three rounds of diamonds, the third was ruffed with dummy's ♠8, and over-ruffed with a deceptive ♠Q.

When Papa exited with a third club and declarer ruffed, Walter, in his usual bovine manner (or whatever manner Walruses have), contributed the ♣K. H.H.'s trance lasted nearly two heartbeats. What was going on in clubs? His natural line would be to try to ruff a fourth diamond, but he surprised everybody by drawing trumps and exiting with a diamond.

As Walter stared at his four remaining cards, he slowly realised that they were all hearts, a suit that he had no intention of leading. His moustache bristled with effort as he struggled to find an alternative, until a braying voice put an end to his agony.

"Don't burst a blood vessel, Walter," chortled the Hog, and mercifully spread his hand.

"Very well played," admitted the author, scribbling furiously. In *Bridge Quarterly*, the hand would read well, especially with himself as declarer.

"You are too kind," demurred H.H. "However, if the hand is to appear in your world-renowned column, please keep my name out of it. The star of the show was my good friend, Themistocles, with his astute false-card of the spade queen. Please make sure you spell his name correctly – it's on the back of his T-shirt."

"I don't know what all the fuss is about," sniffed Molly. "Routine defence, routine declarer play. Happens every day at the Mermaids."

"Then I shan't put it in my next book," retorted the D.B.A. "Since it's clearly the sort of play that turns up more than once a century." He turned his back on Molly and addressed the triumphant Hog.

"How did you judge the distribution so accurately?" he asked. "West might have been dealt four clubs, in which case your plan would have come to a sticky end-play." He made a hasty note of his witticism; it would sound even better in print.

"Once again, I must give credit to my opponent, who is the master of misdirection. That high club on the first round was one of his classic deceptions." H.H. bared his teeth at Papa in what might almost have been a grin. "We Griffins cherish them all. They are as traditional as Christmas, and as predictable as plum pudding."

Luxuriating in the spectacle of Papa silently seething, sulking and smouldering, the Hog warmed to his theme. "These chestnuts remind us of those balmy days when the game was young, and so were we. Nostalgia isn't what it was, and we must cherish every scrap that comes our way. I recall ..."

Educating Papa

Later, Sophia joined the Hog in the bar. As it was their first drink together, it was her turn to pay. "I must speak with you about your four heart contract," she said. "I am sure that my cousin's false-card told you nothing. It was that darling old Walrus who gave the game away."

"True," concurred the Hog. "Reading Walter's face is so easy it makes a Sun headline seem like an intellectual challenge. And the count was beyond doubt when he produced the club king on the third round. W.W. can no more play a false card than Papa can play a true one."

"H.H., you are a wicked man," smiled Sophia. "Why do you make fun of poor Papa?"

"Make fun of Papa?" exploded the Hog. He nipped a heart attack in the bud by gulping down the remains of his champagne cocktail, and waited courteously for Sophia to order another. "If I possess a modicum of skill, is it not my duty to impart it to less...to my fellow players?"

"Yes, but ..." objected S.S., who had not yet learned that the Hog's questions were rhetorical.

"I couldn't agree more," he said. "I confess that on occasions I employ ridicule as an educational weapon. But what is sarcasm but intellect on the offensive? Socrates used it on Plato, Chaucer on Shakespeare. Great teaching has two stages: persuading the student he has a lot to learn, and imparting the requisite knowledge." He paused proudly. "And after a mere decade or two of expert tuition, Papa is already halfway through stage one."

Chapter 8

All Round Brilliance

"I hope you are in the mood to hear a little constructive criticism, Oscar," said Peregrine Penguin, who was the Owl's dinner guest at the Griffins.

"As long as it's about somebody else," responded O.O.

Peregrine took a sip of port, and cleared his throat tactfully. "As you know," he said, "we Unicorns are quite taken with your Millennium venture. Although one category seems to have raised a few eyebrows."

Oscar blinked, taking care not to raise his own eyebrows in the process. "I suspect that you are referring to the Best Played and Defended Hand," he speculated.

"Exactly," nodded P.P. "It presupposes that declarer and both defenders can shine simultaneously. Bearing in mind the wildly variable standard of play at your club – and I freely admit that the Unicorns are no better – is such a coincidence feasible? And since Papa and the Hog are your leading contenders, would either of them allow his name to appear on the same trophy as the other's?"

"Even if they did, it would take them another millennium to agree the billing," remarked O.O. He gazed thirstily at his empty glass. "The port is with you, P.P."

The Penguin murmured an apology and passed the decanter to his host, who was rapidly scanning the pages of his notebook. "Here is a hand that might qualify for the trophy," he said. "Inevitably, the Rueful Rabbit was involved, even though his performance, like Papa's, was flawed. But, as you pointed out earlier, we cannot expect perfection from everyone, so we must make allowances."

Oscar proudly showed the deal to the Penguin, and described the highly charged Griffinesque drama, in which the bidding and play were merely sub-plots.

Love All. Dealer East.

T.T.
♠ 53
♡ AK654
♢ AQJ
♣ AK6

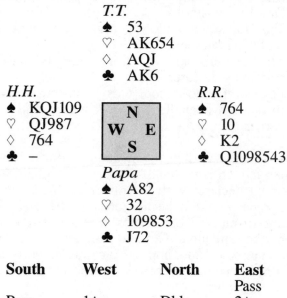

H.H.
♠ KQJ109
♡ QJ987
♢ 764
♣ –

R.R.
♠ 764
♡ 10
♢ K2
♣ Q1098543

Papa
♠ A82
♡ 32
♢ 109853
♣ J72

South	West	North	East
			Pass
Pass	1♠	Dble	2♠
Pass	Pass	Dble	Pass
3♢	Pass	3♡	Pass
3NT	All Pass		

While Papa and the Hideous Hog cut for partners, they exchanged malevolent stares, which gave way to theatrical gasps of relief when H.H. cut the Rabbit and Papa drew the Toucan.

Exercising *droit de seigneur*, Oscar imperiously waved the Corgi to a third row seat, and claimed the chair between the two arch-rivals. However long the rubber, he would always be sitting beside declarer. Sophia the Siren occupied her favourite position, between her cousin and her new idol, the Rabbit.

"Never bid no trumps first," Papa instructed T.T. "And don't be afraid to raise my suits with a good doubleton."

"And remember, Timothy," sniped the Hog. "In the unlikely event of Themistocles supporting your suit, he'll have at least six."

The auction was Standard Griffin. For those not familiar with the subtleties of the system:

1.   R.R. considered opening three clubs, until he recalled
      that H.H. had forbidden him to pre-empt in any of the
      first four positions.
2.   The Hog's one spade was a grotesque underbid, for
      which he later apologised.
3.   The Toucan's bids were bold attempts to avoid
      becoming declarer.
4.   Papa's three no-trumps was so automatic that it was
      made on his behalf by three kibitzers and a passing
      waiter.

The Hog began with two top spades, ducked smoothly by
Papa. Knowing all four hands, Oscar saw that a third round
would present declarer with the contract. With his customary
foresight, Papa would expertly jettison the ♣A. Then, after
establishing diamonds, the Greek would cash dummy's top
hearts, and the remaining diamond honour. Now he would play
the king and another club, hoping to create an entry to his hand.
As the cards lay, he would come to a well-earned nine tricks.

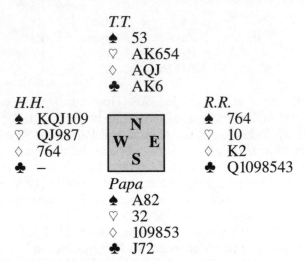

```
                          T.T.
                          ♠ 53
                          ♡ AK654
                          ◊ AQJ
                          ♣ AK6
        H.H.                                    R.R.
        ♠ KQJ109        ┌──────────┐            ♠ 764
        ♡ QJ987         │    N     │            ♡ 10
        ◊ 764           │ W     E  │            ◊ K2
        ♣ –             │    S     │            ♣ Q1098543
                        └──────────┘
                          Papa
                          ♠ A82
                          ♡ 32
                          ◊ 109853
                          ♣ J72
```

    Seeing only two hands, but, as usual, defending double
dummy, the Hog switched to the ♡Q, taken by the ace.
    Oscar, who was in one of his rare, flamboyant moods, was
about to give a faint nod of approval when he saw that Papa

might still succeed. He would cash the ♣A, revealing West's void. Then the ♢A followed by the queen would endplay East, whose best return would be his remaining spade. In an orgy of self-congratulation, Papa would unblock dummy's ♢J, and claim.

A true master in the East position would out-fox the fox by throwing his ♢K on the ace, but when the play proceeded as expected, the Rabbit stolidly produced the ♢2. With a knowing glance at Sophia, Papa cashed dummy's ♡K.

At that moment, Sophia, almost certainly under the influence of the Guardian Angel, decided to cross her long, shapely legs. Hypnotised by the change in position, R.R. failed to notice the change of suit. He was already fingering his ♢K, and it was not until he saw the two red kings side by side on the table, and the black scowl on Papa's face, that he noticed that something was wrong.

"Oh, dear! Er, I thought ... I mean I didn't ... that is ..." he faltered as he braced himself for an avalanche of criticism. But none of his fellow sinners would cast the first stone.

"Why so modest, partner?" sniggered the Hog. "Be like me: never apologise for your brilliancies."

He gleefully recorded fifty above the line, and shook his head at Papa. "But you, Themistocles, should beg Timothy's forgiveness for that superfluous second round of hearts. You were playing R.R. for the diamond king. There was no point in ensuring that hearts were eliminated. Did you really think he had fourteen cards?"

"But I ..." gurgled Papa.

"You snatched defeat from the jaws of victory," suggested the ever-helpful Corgi.

As Papa seethed, Sophia beamed at the Rabbit. "Congratulations," she whispered. "You took your life in your hands when you decided to delay your astute unblock. But you were naughty to play cat and mouse with Themistocles – he has no sense of humour."

She leaned forward to breathe into his long pink ear. "You have a whimsical streak in your nature – are you a Virgo?"

The Corgi maintains to this day that the Rabbit's blush lasted for three rubbers.

Chapter 9

The Game's the Thing

When Oscar had finished his story, P.P. regretfully poured the last of the port. "Papa is so intoxicated with his own ingenuity that he has forgotten the simple art of counting," he said. "But you must admit he was unlucky."

"I admit no such thing," responded Oscar. "Playing that king of hearts was unforgivably careless. He was so contemptuous of R.R.'s skill that he forgot about his supernatural luck."

"The Rabbit has that effect on us," mused Peregrine. "We are like the prize-fighter who drops his guard because his opponent cannot punch, only to discover that his boxing gloves are stuffed with horseshoes."

"I wish I'd said that," admired O.O.

"You will, Oscar, you will," the Penguin comforted him.

The Owl's rejoinder was forestalled by a familiar braying laugh, as the Hideous Hog approached their table, seized an empty chair and, without waiting for anything so trivial as an invitation, placed it between the two Senior Kibitzers.

"Won't you join us?" asked Oscar, a few seconds after the Hog had sat down. "From your obvious good mood, I deduce that you have either won the National Lottery or reduced Themistocles to a quivering jelly."

"You wound me deeply, Oscar," lamented the Hog. "To me, the game is everything. I may derive some small satisfaction from executing a breathtaking coup, but its effect on my opponent is of no importance, whichever Greek ship owner he happens to be. I attribute your uncharitable remark to the emptiness of your decanter. But don't worry, I noticed it on my way in, and asked M. Merle to bring you another. And while we are waiting, here is a hand I am entering for Brilliant Defence."

He produced a final demand for a 1985 tailor's bill, and jotted down two hands:

North/South Game. Dealer East.

Karapet
♠ AJ432
♡ 6
♢ 5
♣ 1098754

H.H.   W.W.
♠ 5
♡ KQJ74   N
♢ K932   W   E
♣ K32   S

Papa

South	West	North	East
			1NT
2♠	4♡	4♠	Pass
Pass	Dble		

"Walter's one no trump showed sixteen to eighteen points. I happened to know it was seventeen, because I watched his lips move as he counted them. I found the perfect lead, my singleton trump. Papa called for the ace; Walter contributed the six. A club was ruffed in hand, and the ace of diamonds was cashed. P.P., perhaps you would like to plan the defence."

The Penguin pursed his lips into a thoughtful beak shape. "There isn't much to plan," he decided. "Declarer will cross-ruff the minors, and it appears that nothing can stop him making the first eight tricks. After that, since W.W. is marked with the vital outstanding honours, Papa will be forced to concede defeat gracefully."

"That Greek has never done anything gracefully in his life," snorted H.H. "But let's have your opinion, Oscar."

By now the port had arrived, together with a bowl of walnuts, which the Hog had thoughtfully requisitioned. While he munched with noisy contentment, O.O. pondered.

"A pity the Toucan isn't here," he concluded. "The problem calls for an unused mind. It is what I call a Mr Macawber hand; you follow suit and wait for something to turn up."

"Which shows how little Jane Austen knew about bridge,"

retorted the Hog. "You are both so concerned with what will happen at trick nine, that you have overlooked the crucial nature of trick three."

Oscar blinked. Peregrine, who was busy with the port, froze in mid-pour. Ever the opportunist, H.H. gently relieved him of the decanter, and topped up his own glass.

"I'll give you a clue," he announced, fifty calories later. "What do you play on Papa's ace of diamonds?"

A glimmer of awareness flickered in the mind of the Owl, but as it refused to crystallise into an intelligent thought, he said nothing.

"Really, Oscar," the Hog interrupted. "I've practically given you the answer on a plate. But let me share my reasoning with you – it's the least I can do, as I'm sharing your port and nuts. The moment I saw dummy, I knew that Papa had overcalled on wafer-thin values. Once the ace of diamonds appeared, I could almost deduce his exact holding, which I will now reveal, while Peregrine kindly replenishes my glass."

He pencilled in the South and East hands:

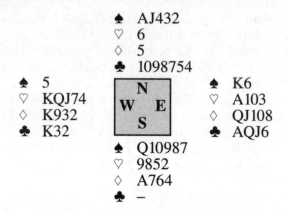

```
              ♠ AJ432
              ♡ 6
              ◇ 5
              ♣ 1098754
♠ 5              N            ♠ K6
♡ KQJ74      W     E          ♡ A103
◇ K932           S            ◇ QJ108
♣ K32                         ♣ AQJ6
              ♠ Q10987
              ♡ 9852
              ◇ A764
              ♣ –
```

"Note what happens if you play thoughtlessly," H.H. proceeded. "Papa must place West with the king of diamonds and crossruff until that card appears. When it does, instead of ruffing, he discards dummy's singleton heart. With West having no trump to lead, declarer must come to nine trump tricks plus the diamond ace."

With Old World courtesy, the Hog masticated some more

nuts, to allow his audience a chance to catch up. Noting their awed silence, he resumed his flow.

"That is why, on the diamond ace, I pitched my king. Papa, who is a good enough technician to plan that scissors coup, but not to find the defence to it, was stupefied. But did he offer his congratulations, as I would have done had the positions been reversed?"

"Off the top of my head, I would say not," reflected the Owl, with a perfectly straight face. "But I'm sure your partner ..."

"Bah!" snarled H.H. "That Walrus knows no more about bridge than I do about Bolivian basket weaving. All he could do was demand why, with a total of twenty-nine points, we only got them one down. As if it was my fault!"

"And Karapet?" prompted Oscar, hoping for an opportunity to grab a stray walnut.

"Need you ask?" lamented the Hog. "He claimed the entire credit for Papa's defeat. Apparently it was due to the Witch of Arrowroot casting a spell on the Djoulikyans in 1492. They were on their way to America at the time, but because of her, some Spanish fellow beat them to it." He took a medicinal gulp, and continued mournfully. "My superb defence was like Byron's blushing flower, wasting its sweetness on the desert storm."

"But surely one or two of my students ..." began the Owl sympathetically.

"They were all at another table, kibitzing Papa's cousin, who was kibitzing the Rabbit. And I blame you for that, Oscar. These youngsters ..."

The Owl regarded the accusing pink forefinger with a jaundiced eye. The Hog had gone too far, and Oscar vowed to make him regret it.

"You have my sympathy, H.H.," he purred dangerously. "The rules of the Millennium Competition require that each entry must have been witnessed by a non-combatant. But I'm sure you'll come up with another brilliant defence which will thrill the committee."

He seized the decanter from the paralysed Hog, and helped himself generously. "Anyway, as you yourself said, the game's the thing."

Chapter 10

The Birthday Boy

"Can I help you with that oyster?" asked the Hog.

"No, thank you, H.H.," replied the Rabbit. "I'm quite capable of opening it."

"I was thinking more in terms of eating it," said H.H. "You know how much they upset your digestion."

R.R.'s birthday was always one of the great events of the Griffins' social calendar. The Rabbit was so popular, and so generous, that he celebrated three birthdays a year, each of them marked by a lavish dinner party. For the last occasion before the Millennium, he invited the Toucan, the Owl and the Corgi, three of his most frequent guests, and the Hog, who could more accurately be described as permanent.

The conversational skills of the five were so wide-ranging that it was nearly a minute before the subject of bridge was mentioned. Colin the Corgi looked very pleased with himself as he showed everyone the West and North hands of one of the day's deals.

"You were my partner, Timothy," he reminded the Toucan. "But I know I can trust you not to give the game away."

"Certainly," promised T.T., trying to look like a man whose memory reached back nearly two hours, and failing miserably when he realised that he did not recall any of the events which the Corgi described:

Love All. Dealer South.

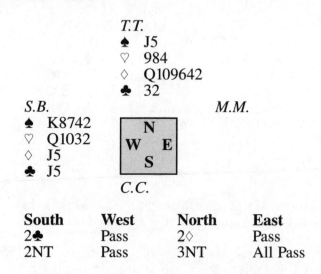

T.T.
♠ J5
♡ 984
◇ Q109642
♣ 32

S.B.
♠ K8742
♡ Q1032
◇ J5
♣ J5

M.M.

C.C.

South	West	North	East
2♣	Pass	2◇	Pass
2NT	Pass	3NT	All Pass

The Emeritus Professor of Bio-Sophistry selected a scholarly four of spades for his opening lead. Molly won with the ace, Colin contributing the three, and smartly returned the ♠10, which was covered by C.C.'s queen.

Crossing his long spindly legs, S.B. tugged one of the tufts of hair which protruded from his ears, a sure sign that his sharp legal brain was in top gear.

There were two distributions consistent with the play. Molly the Mule might be starting to unblock from ♠A1096, in which case it would be imperative to win the trick. On the other hand, if she had been dealt ♠A106, it would be necessary to duck.

After weighing the evidence, S.B. took with his king and returned a low spade. His expression, when Molly won with the nine and the Corgi amazingly followed suit, was a study in judicial disbelief. She had no more spades to lead!

"I don't believe it," he muttered.

"I do," carped the Mule, as she returned a heart, more in anger than in hope.

This was the full deal:

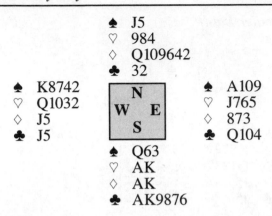

```
              ♠ J5
              ♡ 984
              ◇ Q109642
              ♣ 32
♠ K8742                      ♠ A109
♡ Q1032        N             ♡ J765
◇ J5        W     E          ◇ 873
♣ J5           S             ♣ Q104
              ♠ Q63
              ♡ AK
              ◇ AK
              ♣ AK9876
```

Colin the Corgi gleefully won the Mule's heart switch, cashed two clubs and cleared the suit. He now had nine top tricks.

"I may disagree with your play, Professor," he misquoted. "But I will defend to the death your right to play it."

"Why on earth didn't you duck the queen of spades?" demanded Molly.

"Not being telepathic, I had no way of knowing the spade distribution," argued the Secretary Bird.

"Well, I would have ducked," asserted Molly.

"Congratulations." S.B. curled his lip into a sardonic smile. "But without the benefit of your woman's intuition, I was forced to rely on mere male logic. Had I let declarer hold the trick, he might have been able to run the diamonds and cash out. Furthermore, had you been dealt the ace, ten and six, you would surely have inserted the ten at trick one. Therefore ..."

"Typical," sniffed Molly. "When a man is in the wrong, he always hides behind a load of whys and wherefores and furthermores. Fancy falling for a baby deception like that."

"I'm sorry," mocked the Corgi. "But from the vantage point of my perambulator it appeared that there were no adult deceptions available. My only hope was to induce the defence to block the spades, and had I played low your partner would certainly have ducked."

"Really?" countered Molly. "I suppose you think I can't analyse a bridge hand, hardly know one card from another, and ought to bow down to clever young men from Oxbridge."

The Corgi considered this at some length. "Close," he admitted.

A Compliment from H.H.

Having concluded his recital and praised himself sufficiently, C.C. passed the diagram to Oscar. "A possibility for a Deceptive Play prize?" he solicited.

"I couldn't possibly comment," the Owl ducked smoothly. "My official position, you understand."

"I would have ducked," announced R.R., reaching for his full sherry glass, only to find that it had been replaced mysteriously by the Hog's empty one. "You see, the king of spades is the card I would normally play, so it must be the wrong one, mustn't it? I mean, er ..."

"Quite so, R.R.," interjected H.H. "I too would have let Colin hold the trick, but for a different reason. After making the dubious assumption that from ace-ten-six, Molly would have inserted the ten, S.B. overlooked a more telling one."

He paused to seize the last of the canapés, beating the Owl's swoop by a millimetre. "In my rare uncharitable moments, I have accused Molly of many things, but never of being a bridge player. Yet she usually makes laydown contracts, which puts her in a higher bracket than the Walrus. And like Walter, she knows a few simple rules, and follows them slavishly. Holding ace-ten-nine-six, she would return the six."

Oozing benevolence from every follicle, he regarded the Corgi. "You came to that conclusion, Colin, which is why you were able to place West with a five-card spade suit and bring off your neat deception."

"Thank you," replied the Corgi suspiciously. The Hog was after something, but what?

"Not at all," responded the Hog. "I always give credit where it is due. Although in Oscar's position, I wouldn't go as far as to give you the prize, which I understand is a dozen bottles of *Krug*. But I'm sure that the winner, whoever he may be, will generously present you with one of mi– that is to say, his."

"But surely ..." remonstrated C.C., though he didn't really mean it.

"I disagree," contradicted the Hog, purely as a matter of form. "But I would certainly award you a medal for Unselfish Bidding. Your willingness to attempt an unmakeable contract, to spare Timothy the stress of struggling in an unbeatable diamond game, was heroic."

He paused for a brief stuffed olive break, and beamed at his audience. "Would you like me to tell you a story?"

Nobody objected. Another tray of canapés had arrived, and a peroration from H.H. might give them a sporting chance of getting one apiece.

A Royal Swindle

"Once upon a time," recited the Hog, "there was a king, who had to choose between two brilliant candidates for the post of court painter."

"I love stories," squawked the Toucan, bouncing in his seat. "Which one did he choose?"

"He decided to appoint the man who could produce the most realistic still life. On the day of judgement, the competing canvasses were displayed in the palace garden, and concealed behind red, velvet curtains. When the first candidate pulled the golden curtain cord, he revealed a bowl of cherries, so realistic that a hungry bird flew down and tried to devour them."

The Hog paused, not for dramatic effect, but to lay claim to the last of the smoked salmon and caviar.

"There was a burst of applause from the royal kibitzers," he continued. "The result seemed a formality, but when the bird had flown away, having discovered that paint-flavoured canvas was inedible, the second aspirant stood in front of his painting and invited the monarch himself to unveil it. But as the king attempted to do so, he discovered to his amazement that the subject of the masterpiece was a red velvet curtain with a golden cord."

"Bravo!" cried the Owl and the Corgi, and the Hog was about to take a bow, when he realised that they were applauding the arrival of a magnum of *Veuve Clicquot*.

"But who won?" cried Timothy the Toucan.

"Don't worry, Timothy," the Corgi reassured him. "I'm sure

they all lived happily ever after. But tell me something, H.H..
What exactly is the connection between your fairy tale and my
coup?"

"The quality of a deception must be measured against the
quality of its victim," the Hog informed him. "Like you, the first
painter only managed to fool a bird."

He seized one of the Rabbit's birthday cards, which were
discreetly arranged on the dining table, and began to scribble a
deal. "Now here is a coup which might have deceived a king.
Anyway, it fooled Themistocles, who I suppose we can class
amongst the minor nobility."

Game All. Dealer North.

Anonymous Griffin
♠ KQ104
♡ A752
◇ K92
♣ KQ

H.H.   *C.C.*

	N	
W		E
	S	

Papa
♠ A5
♡ Q109864
◇ 876
♣ 52

South	West	North	East
		1NT	Pass
4♡	All Pass		

"I've been saving this hand for your birthday, R.R.," he told
the grateful Rabbit. "I hope you haven't already got one.
Anyway, I led the jack of clubs. Colin took with the ace and
returned the three. You are in the dummy. How should you
proceed?"

"I've been reading a book," twittered the Rabbit excitedly.

"*Fifty Tips for Beg–* er, *Bridge Players*. It says that there are a lot of people sleeping under the embankment because they didn't draw trumps."

"Really?" drawled the Corgi. "Is that a bridge tip, or an ad for a cheap night's lodging?"

"I don't care," retorted R.R., tipsily holding out his glass for more champagne. "I'm going to cash my ace of trumps and see what happens."

"Papa must have read the same book," the Hog informed him. "But, being Papa, he had to find a clever way of doing it. He didn't want to let me in to make a killing diamond switch. So he crossed to his ace of spades, and led…Oscar, which heart do you think Papa chose?"

"The queen," declared the Owl promptly. "Although it depends how many people were watching."

"A goodly number," stated the Hog. "So the queen it was. When my knave appeared, he posed hammily for his audience, and who can blame him? To such a master technician, the deal was an open book. He spread his hand and took a well deserved curtain call."

"I needn't dot the i's and cross the t's," he said, and proceeded to do so. He told us how he would go up with dummy's ace and throw Colin in with the king. He explained in minute detail that any lead my partner made would give him his tenth trick.

"And did it?" asked the Rabbit breathlessly.

"It would have done." The Hog's small pink eyes twinkled smugly. "But, unfortunately for Themistocles, it was I who held the trump king."

"Superb," said the Owl, referring to the *Veuve Clicquot*.

"Magnificent," corrected the Hog, referring to his play. "Let me show you the full deal. You might like to have it framed."

He filled in the East and West hands with the complacent air of Pablo Picasso polishing off his morning master-work.

"When Themistocles produced his spade ace," he said, "I knew that the contract was cold, unless, of course, I contrived a routine miracle. And here it is."

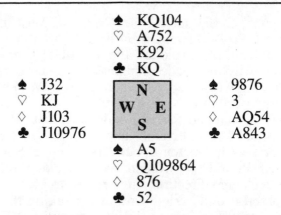

♠ KQ104
♥ A752
◇ K92
♣ KQ

♠ J32   ♠ 9876
♥ KJ   ♥ 3
◇ J103   ◇ AQ54
♣ J10976   ♣ A843

♠ A5
♥ Q109864
◇ 876
♣ 52

"It goes without saying that I could tell every card in Papa's hand, or every card that mattered. So my bizarre play of the knave was quite sound."

"But he might have had a diamond honour," objected O.O.

"Come, come, Oscar," remonstrated the Hog. "Has our long association taught you nothing? Had Papa held a diamond honour, the contract would have been a laydown, provided he made the standard safety play in hearts, and he would never have led that flamboyant queen, even if all the world was watching."

"Then Papa was truly unlucky," murmured the Owl. "Congratulations, H.H. The play of the heart knave would have deceived the king. Or, may I say it? Even yourself."

"True," the Hog agreed, not from modesty, but from a desire for the *Krug*. "Although I would still make the contract." He paused to relish Oscar's hoot of amazement, the Rabbit's squeak of hero worship, and the puzzled frown of the Toucan, who was still pondering over the cryptic fable.

"Papa couldn't resist giving Colin three ways of conceding the contract," explained H.H. "I would have been content with two. Yes, I too would have placed C.C. with the king of hearts, but I would have taken the precaution of eliminating the spades first. As the cards lay, this would have given me ten tricks."

He poured the last of the champagne and, with a meaningful glare at his host, placed the bottle upside down in the ice bucket. "I shall dot no i's, I shall cross no t's," he said. "I shall let the quality of my dummy play speak for itself."

Oscar was deeply moved. "I take it that you showed the same

noble reticence at the table," he said. "It must have been tempting to tell Papa where he went wrong."

"Oh, he told him!" exploded the Corgi. "He gave him so many reasons why the spade elimination was necessary, that I stopped counting when the total reached fifty. We'd played five more rubbers by the time he'd finished."

"*Mea culpa*," intoned the Hog solemnly. "But the seeds of knowledge should be cultivated in public, as Doctor Johnson remarked, or was it Doctor Spock? No matter. Some people maintain that Papa has travelled too far along the road to mediocrity to change direction, but I refuse to give up hope."

"I've worked it out!" cried Timothy, breaking the profound silence. They stared at him in polite incredulity. "The winner was the one who painted the nice bowl of fruit. It's all very well to paint a pair of curtains, but who would buy a picture like that?"

Chapter 11

World Rankings

"Fame is the perfume of heroic deeds."

The Hideous Hog was in a listening mood. Lounging in the bar with the Corgi, the Owl and the Walrus, he listened contentedly to a rich resonant voice, waxing eloquent on the subject of famous bridge players. Much of his pleasure derived from the fact that the voice was his own.

"It never ceases to amaze me that Bob Hamman is ranked as the world's best player," he complained. "Don't get me wrong – he has no greater admirer than me. Why, he often plays difficult contracts exactly as I would. But I refuse to accept him as a hero until he proves himself at the most challenging level."

"What do you mean?" demanded the Walrus. "I don't know much about the fellow, but hasn't he won umpteen world championships?"

"Irrelevant." The Hog waved Oscar's cigar dismissively. "With the Meckwell machine in the other room, and Wolff or Soloway opposite, I would have won umpteen plus one, provided they let me play the contracts. As it is, I am invariably saddled with the Rabbit and the Toucan and Walter, I do believe it's your round."

"Tell us, H.H.," asked the Corgi. "If Hamman isn't *Numero Uno*, are you claiming that honour for yourself?"

"I shouldn't dream of it," demurred the Hog. "It is possible that in some far country there is another, of comparable talent, who also prefers the obscurity of high-stake rubber bridge, and is immune to the lure of fame and poverty. I will go further: there may be several of us."

The others shuddered at the prospect of the existence of other Hogs. The world no longer seemed a safe place. They unconsciously edged closer to each other to form a protective triangle.

Scribbling rapidly on Oscar's drinks coaster, H.H. deftly confiscated the Owl's Madeira in the process. "Here is a hand I played against you, Colin. I know you enjoyed it; it gave you a chance to show what a good loser you were."

North/South Game. Dealer East.

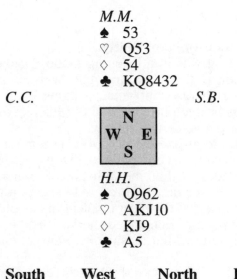

M.M.
♠ 53
♡ Q53
♢ 54
♣ KQ8432

C.C.   S.B.

H.H.
♠ Q962
♡ AKJ10
♢ KJ9
♣ A5

South	West	North	East
			Pass
2NT	Pass	3NT	All Pass

"You opened two no-trumps with an eighteen count!" expostulated the Walrus.

"You've forgotten H.H.'s system, Walter," elucidated C.C. "He adds so many points for his dummy play that it was actually a gross underbid. But it had the merit of right-siding the contract."

"Absolutely," confirmed the Hog. "In deference to Molly's feminist principles, I never open a door for her, or offer her my seat. On the rare occasions that she joins us for a drink, I graciously let her pay. But I am too much of a gentleman to subject a member of the gentle sex (or in her case an associate member) to the indignity of botching a contract that I would make in my sleep. I can't change – it's a matter of upbringing."

Seeing that the barman had placed a bowl of cashew nuts within easy reach, he motioned the Corgi to pursue the narrative.

"I led the jack of spades," said Colin. "S.B. took with the king and continued with ace and another. H.H. won with the queen, I followed and ..." He broke off to decipher the Hog's frantic nut-hampered mumblings. "I believe that our hero is defying you to suggest the winning line."

Walter the Walrus plunged intrepidly into the breach. "Straightforward hand," he said. "No sense in fiddling about – start on the clubs. Mind you, I know they won't break – I wasn't born yesterday, you know. But even so, I still have eight top tricks."

"Gripping stuff, Walter, but where will your ninth come from?" enquired C.C. "To help you decide, let's suppose that East shows up with four clubs."

Walter shrugged. He had worked hard for his eight tricks. Now it was up to Oscar to tie up the loose ends.

"Clearly it's time to play a diamond from the table," suggested the Owl. "Though if declarer misguesses he could be two off. But I take it that H.H., by a feat of inspired logic, got it right. Of course, as he reminds us every day and twice on Sundays, he never guesses."

Having removed the threat of imminent starvation, the Hog was ready to reclaim the centre stage. "I do not believe in guessing until I have all the relevant data," he told them. "The best way of extracting it was to cash my winning hearts. When *Colin* followed to four rounds, the contract was as good as bankable."

Oscar's incredulous hoot was accompanied by a sceptical snort from Walter, who didn't believe in clairvoyance.

"All I had to do was to cash the ace of clubs, exit with a spade, and claim. You all know how much I deplore ostentation, but it saves time, which on an average day is worth a pound a minute. Let me show you the East/West hands, although, by now, even a player with half a brain should have deduced every significant card."

He directed a smile of enquiry at the Walrus, who nodded affirmatively.

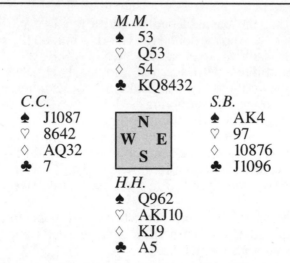

M.M.
♠ 53
♡ Q53
◇ 54
♣ KQ8432

C.C.
♠ J1087
♡ 8642
◇ AQ32
♣ 7

S.B.
♠ AK4
♡ 97
◇ 10876
♣ J1096

H.H.
♠ Q962
♡ AKJ10
◇ KJ9
♣ A5

"When I threw Colin in with a spade, he had nothing to lead but diamonds," began the Hog.

"But you didn't know that at the time," carped Walter. "If he exits with a club, bang goes your fancy plan. That's the trouble with you experts, sometimes you're too clever for your own good."

"If Colin has a second club, my dear Walter, the suit is almost certain to break," countered the Hog. "You're an accountant – count his hand. He's already shown up with four cards in each major. If he also holds four clubs, that would place him with one diamond, and East with seven. If they included the ace, he would have opened one diamond. So if by some miracle Colin plays a second club and the suit turns out to be four-one, I can leave a club winner in dummy and play a diamond to the nine, forcing his bare ace."

He paused to allow Walter time to audit his calculations, and turned triumphantly towards the Owl "Not a difficult hand, Oscar. On one of his good days, even Papa would have found the right line, so naturally I shan't submit it for a prize. But admit it, O.O., Bob Hamman would never have made three no trumps."

This was too much for the honest Owl, who had been one of Hamman's guest kibitzers on several occasions. "H.H.!" he spluttered.

"You are missing the point, Oscar," said the Hog. "Hamman

would have opened the bidding with an unimaginative one of something. Poor Molly would have responded one no trump, and subsequently gone down in three. And what kind of hero would use a member of the fair sex as a shield against his enemies?"

He seized the last of the cashew nuts and crunched contemptuously "World Number One?" he laughed derisively. "He's not even a gentleman."

The Hog as Dummy

A thousand words, and almost as many calories, later, the Hog revisited his theme of world rankings.

"I hear that as well as being a fine bidder and – let's give the fellow his due – an adequate card player, our world number one is a model partner. Presumably this means he is charming, sympathetic, tactful and trusting, all the qualities for losing a fortune at the Griffins. Can you imagine trusting the Rabbit to land a small slam with only twelve tricks?"

"Well, I've watched you raise him into several slams," demurred O.O.

"That doesn't mean he trusts R.R. to play them," remarked the Corgi. "Let me give you an example from yesterday. It shows the Hog at the peak of his towering brilliance. He gave new meaning to the phrase 'dummy play'."

He looked round for a piece of paper, and the Hog, always charitable to somebody who was about to sing his praises, donated his latest letter of admonishment from the club committee.

This was the deal the Corgi described, with sardonic relish:

North/South Game. Dealer South.

H.H.
♠ A10964
♡ J105
◇ Q10
♣ AK2

S.B.
♠ 8
♡ KQ73
◇ K76
♣ QJ1043

```
    N
 W     E
    S
```

W.W.
♠ 72
♡ 42
◇ 98532
♣ 9765

R.R.
♠ KQJ53
♡ A986
◇ AJ4
♣ 8

South	West	North	East
1♠	Dble	2NT	Pass
3♡	Pass	4♠	Pass
4NT	Pass	5♡	Pass
6♠	All Pass		

Having memorised *Playing the Dummy,* a work which seemed to have been written with him in mind, the Rabbit examined the Hog's collection with an air of baffled certainty. He even began the painful task of counting his tricks. There were five spades, two clubs and one club ruff, two diamonds and one heart. Eleven! And the twelfth would materialise after a spot of elimination followed by a perfect page thirty-six end play.

With the courage born of ignorance, R.R. renounced his vow never to claim a contract until he had made an overtrick. "The finesses will all be wrong, but it doesn't matter, because I won't take them," he explained proudly. "After stripping the black suits, ruffing out the clubs and drawing trumps, that is, I shall run the jack of hearts. That's not really a finesse, it's a ... er ... total elimination, and I shan't need to repeat it. Whatever S.B. does will give me an extra trick in one of the black suits."

"That is true, but I still make it one down," sibilated S.B.

"You have only ten top tricks, and your end play will yield another. But I am afraid ten plus one does not make twelve."

R.R. blushed with shame as he recounted. He was used to going down, but not in such a humiliating fashion.

"Professor!" thundered the Hog. "Are you trying to bamboozle my partner out of a cold slam, when he has told you precisely how he is going to make it?"

"If you imagine I will allow myself to be squeezed," challenged S.B., "then think again. I will return whichever red suit declarer discards on the king of clubs."

"I am sure that you are right, Professor," replied H.H. dangerously. "But in the interests of justice, the hand must be played out in the manner indicated by my er ... inspired partner."

The Rabbit, with head bowed, dutifully ruffed a club with the ♠J and crossed to the ♠9. He now led the ♣K, but he had no idea what to do next until the Hog purred his next instruction:

"Having stated that you would ruff out the clubs, that is what you must do."

S.B.'s pince-nez glittered malignantly, but he was too angry to spot a suitable loophole, precedent or grounds for dismissal. After ruffing with his ♠K, R.R. overtook the ♠Q with dummy's ace. Now, in accordance with his statement, he ran the ♡J.

This was the position after the Secretary Bird captured the trick:

```
                  ♠  1064
                  ♡  105
                  ◇  Q10
                  ♣  —
   ♠  —          ┌─────────┐      ♠  —
   ♡  K73        │    N    │      ♡  2
   ◇  K76        │  W   E  │      ◇  98532
   ♣  J          │    S    │      ♣  9
                 └─────────┘
                  ♠  5
                  ♡  A98
                  ◇  AJ4
                  ♣  —
```

At this point, the killing defence was a club. Declarer would have been able to throw a heart from hand, but would have been barred from taking the subsequent ruffing finesse. But S.B., fated never to benefit from law-enforcement, stolidly exited with a small diamond, taken by dummy's queen.

"Now R.R.," advised the Hog, "you must play another heart, foregoing the finesse, as you promised." He leered at S.B., who wanted to disagree, but could barely manage to stop himself nodding judicially.

After the mesmerised Rabbit had played a heart to his ace, H.H. gave his final command. "To comply with the last letter of the law, partner, all you may now do is cash winners. So go to it!"

R.R. began to reel off his trumps, to leave this position when the last trump was led:

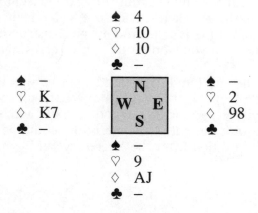

```
              ♠  4
              ♡  10
              ◇  10
              ♣  −

♠  −                        ♠  −
♡  K        N               ♡  2
◇  K7    W     E            ◇  98
♣  −        S               ♣  −

              ♠  −
              ♡  9
              ◇  AJ
              ♣  −
```

When declarer discarded his last heart, S.B. was caught in a simple squeeze, but refused to lose hope. Casually parting with the ◇7, he prayed for the Rabbit to make a mistake, which judging by his bewildered expression was not unlikely.

While R.R. plunged into a cataleptic trance, the Hog demonstrated a level of partnership understanding never before witnessed at the club or anywhere else. He yawned, he drummed his fingers on the table, he looked at his watch. Then, as soon as he judged that the Rabbit had reached the maximum point of irritation, he allowed a predatory pink finger to hover over the ♡10.

With a shrill of defiance, R.R. thrust aside the offending digit and contrarily seized the ◊10, fully prepared for an honourable defeat, rather than a Hog-assisted victory.

"You know how I hate it when you do that," he complained, and was about to play his ◊J when the pink finger returned to wag reprovingly.

"Remember your statement, partner. No finesses," chortled H.H.

When the Professor's ◊K fell under the ace, R.R. squeaked in amazement.

"What happened?" he gurgled.

At the conclusion of Colin's narration, Oscar the Owl, still simmering at the Hog's cavalier treatment of his letter of admonishment, opened his mouth to deliver a stern lecture, but was forestalled by the Hog at his most rampant.

"Don't talk about ethics, Oscar," he scoffed. "I observed the laws of bridge to the letter. My interpretation of one or two of them may have been … somewhat creative, but it has long been a tradition of British justice to allow counsel for the defence a certain amount of latitude."

He allowed himself the latitude of sampling Oscar's house claret and courteously returned the empty glass to its owner.

"Besides," he added, "I owed it to my partner to atone for my failure to right-side the slam, though it wasn't easy after he opened my suit. But, on reflection, I may have misjudged Hamman. Having read his book, I will concede that after a month or so at the Griffins he might well learn to play the Rabbit's contracts as well as I do."

Chapter 12

Things That Go Bump in the Night

"When I was a young man," recalled Oscar the Owl, whose long memory was a byword, "I was a confirmed sceptic. I scoffed at all things supernatural. I walked under ladders with impunity, and laughed when black cats crossed my path. I never touched wood, or crossed my fingers. I was also an atheist, and I thanked God for it." He gave his head a self-deprecating shake. "In short, I was a pompous fool."

"And what changed you?" enquired Peregrine Penguin, not out of curiosity, but to show that he accepted his guest's choice of tense.

"The Griffins," replied the Owl sombrely. "I now believe in the fourth dimension – the Hog is continually popping in and out of it to discover hitherto unknown coups. And when you see Karapet and the Rabbit struggling in the grip of unseen forces, why even you must ..."

"Not I," protested P.P. "I refuse to believe in fairies; I'm a Unicorn. Have another glass of Madeira, it is bound to cheer you up."

"Thank you. I will, but it won't. What natural explanation can there be for the coincidences that abound at the Griffins? In most clubs, criss-cross squeezes and smother-plays turn up three or four times a year at most. Yet they are practically our staple diet. Our classic deals recur with a frequency that sets the laws of probability at nought. And when Karapet's Witch joins forces with the Rabbit's Guardian Angel ..."

Despite himself Peregrine shivered. He needed no psychic powers to predict two things. He was about to hear a story, and it would be a long one. But like the good host that he was, he sat back and thought of England, as Oscar related his tale of Gothic horror:

North/South Game. Dealer South.

D.D.
♠ 1062
♡ KQJ987
♢ KJ
♣ 98

W.W.
♠ QJ94
♡ A32
♢ Q1084
♣ 42

```
      N
   W     E
      S
```

R.R.
♠ —
♡ 10654
♢ 96532
♣ 10763

Karapet
♠ AK8753
♡ —
♢ A7
♣ AKQJ5

South	West	North	East
2♠	Pass	3♡	Pass
4♣	Pass	4♠	Pass
5♢	Pass	5♠	Pass
6♠	Dble	Pass	Pass
6NT	Dble	All Pass	

Fearing that his opponents might overcall in hearts, Karapet chose to open with a strong Acol two spades, rather than a game forcing two clubs. After an auction which suggested that there was intelligent life on earth, he reached an excellent spade slam, but when Walter's fatuous double warned him that it was doomed, switched to no trumps. There was no escape. With or despite the bit between his teeth, the Walrus doubled with a Wagnerian roar, and led the ♠Q.

Expecting the worst, the Free Armenian regarded the Rabbit's diamond discard with practised stoicism. The battle was as good as lost, but he vowed to go down fighting. If he led a small spade towards the ten, he would get out for one down, which for a Djoulikyan would be a major victory.

Then, as he stared mournfully at Dolly the Dove's dummy, it came to him in a flash that the hand bore an uncanny resemblance to one that H.H. had played on a transatlantic cruise. Both the Hog and the Griffin's Chronicle had been full of it for weeks. The only difference was that dummy's long suit had been a significantly more solid KQJ1098. H.H. had taken the first trick, successfully finessed the ◊J, and thrown his ◊A on the ♡K. Now, whatever West led would create an entry to the table. Sheer magic.

But now the wicked Witch had struck again, tantalising him beyond endurance by withholding that precious ♡10. With nine top tricks in the other suits, he needed three more in hearts. Unless the ten was doubleton or tripleton, the Hog's line would fail.

What were the chances? In view of the Rabbit's first discard, his most likely shape was 0-4-5-4, in which case the odds were heavily in favour of R.R. holding ♡10xxx.

There was one ray of hope. Karapet squared his shoulders, gritted his teeth, crossed his fingers, said his prayers, and finessed the ◊J. It held! Now he was ready for a swindle worthy of Papa, or even the Hog. It might not succeed against an alert player, but it was bound to fool the innocent Rabbit. So with a casual air, he called for dummy's ♡7!

Equally casually, R.R. produced the ♡10. He looked vaguely surprised when it held, but fortuitously returned a diamond. Now Karapet could manage only nine tricks. Even worse, a brilliancy prize had slipped through his fingers.

"Why does this always happen to me?" he wailed. "You had no right to play your ten of hearts. It was the correct card!"

"I know it was," retorted the Rabbit, quivering with indignation. "I've been reading a book, *Fifty Tips for Beg–* er, *Advanced Players*. And tip thirty-seven is 'Always signal with the highest card you can afford', so I did."

Karapet's eyes rolled heavenwards. "And what on earth were you signalling?" he demanded.

"Length. I wanted to show Walter I had an even number."

"And it worked," declared the Walrus. "That's why I was able to plan that defence which got you three down. R.R.'s signal gave me a count of not only your hand but my own. You academic chaps are so busy thinking up complicated plans that you forget the most important thing of all. Signalling!"

Murphy's Law

"Well?" Oscar challenged the Penguin when his tale was told. "Can you put that down to coincidence?"

"I can and I do," asserted P.P. "I place the Witch and the Angel in the same category as Santa Claus and the Tooth Fairy."

"Then come and visit us tomorrow," said O.O. "It happens to be Karapet's birthday, and the Witch is bound to cook up something extra special. And I shall make sure that he is matched against the Rabbit."

On the following evening, it was a simple matter for the puissant Owl to manoeuvre Karapet and the Rabbit to the same well-placed table. He relied on the forces of light and darkness to see that they opposed each other, by controlling the cut, and was not disappointed.

R.R. faced the peace-loving Dolly the Dove, and with Sophia the Siren at his side, he seemed unstoppable. Karapet drew Papa.

At the Greek's right, waiting to cut in, sat the Hideous Hog, torn between the hope that the rubber would end quickly, and the delicious expectation that the face of his archenemy would soon be disfigured by large quantities of self-inflicted egg.

But other-worldly powers were abroad on that fateful winter night, and the Greek was to play but a minor part in the melodrama.

After each side had made a deadly dull game, Peregrine cocked a dubious eyebrow at Oscar. The Great Kibitzer responded by raising an admonishing finger, as if to convey that the Witch and the G.A. were merely creating a lull before the inevitable storm.

They were.

It broke on the third hand, dealt without incident by the Rueful Rabbit.

Game All. Dealer East.

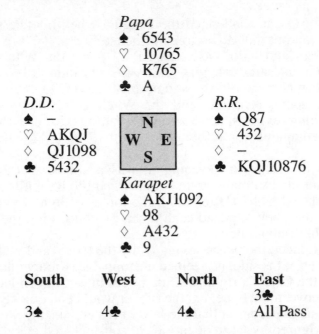

Papa
♠ 6543
♡ 10765
◇ K765
♣ A

D.D.
♠ –
♡ AKQJ
◇ QJ1098
♣ 5432

R.R.
♠ Q87
♡ 432
◇ –
♣ KQJ10876

Karapet
♠ AKJ1092
♡ 98
◇ A432
♣ 9

South	West	North	East
			3♣
3♠	4♣	4♠	All Pass

Of course, Dolly the Dove should have bid five clubs. With twelve certain tricks, the Rabbit might only have gone one down But her eyes, as though compelled by powerful unseen forces, were drawn to Karapet's long mournful nose, which, for some reason, reminded her that it was the poor man's birthday.

With a soft coo of charity, she passed and led her ♡AKQ. Karapet ruffed the third round and laid down his ♠A. He crossed to the ♣A, but before taking the marked finesse in trumps, he paused for reflection. He could count nine top tricks and the tenth seemed to depend on diamonds breaking three-two. Rejecting Euclidean mathematics in favour of the more reliable Djoulikyan variety, he calculated that 5-0 was far more likely. Besides, with the Rabbit showing up with three cards in each major, his distribution was marked.

The key play came to him in a blinding flash. Like all the truly great masochists from Job to Murphy[1], Karapet spent his long lonely nights wallowing not only in his own disasters but the triumphs of the more fortunate. The deal was identical to

---

[1] Murphy's Law: *Anything that can go wrong will go wrong.*
Karapet's Law: *Murphy was an optimist.*

another classic from the Griffins' rich history, which saw the Rabbit at the helm.

Karapet recollected that, after successfully negotiating the trump finesse, R.R. had inadvertently led the ♠9 from hand, throwing R.H.O. in with the ♠Q. East had nothing to lead but a club, so declarer discarded a diamond from hand, and ruffed in dummy. Then, for want of anything better to do, he led out his trumps. It transpired that the unnatural loss of a trump trick had not only forced the ruff and discard, it had rectified the count for a red-suit squeeze against West. It was a splendid coup, for the trick had to be lost to East. Had declarer ducked a diamond, West could have broken up the squeeze by returning the ♡J.

Now Karapet, who could remember every word of the Griffins' Chronicle, was about to replicate the coup despite the machinations of the Wicked Witch of Ararat.

He played a club to the ace, and, cackling with contempt, he led one of dummy's small spades, but froze with horror when the Rabbit's queen appeared!

The Armenian refused to accept defeat. On the theory that R.R. may have placed a spade in with his clubs, he let the queen hold, hoping for a ruff and discard. But R.R. exited with his trump and two diamonds had to be lost. Two off.

The deadly Rabbit punch defied comment, and Sophia was the first to make one.

"*Olé*!" she cried. "I salute you, Karapet, for your superb play, and you, my friend R.R., for your astute riposte. It was a memorable battle of wits."

"Memorable?" snorted the Hog. "I bet it's a battle Karapet might prefer to forget, although it was brave of him to turn up for it completely unarmed."

"Are you suggesting …?" cried Karapet.

"I am," snarled the Hog. "You should have ruffed the third heart with your knave. That deuce was a precious asset, and you squandered it shamelessly."

Karapet was shaken, but not stirred. A moment's thought confirmed that the Hog was right. But nobody could possibly have foreseen the need for such an unlikely safety play. Nobody, that is, except a Guardian Angel who was a fusion of a dozen deceased world champions. Or the Hideous Hog himself. He needed no guardian angel – he was in league with the Devil. He probably was the Devil!

A Bar Room Brawl

On the next deal, the Rabbit made three no trumps with a smother play. Karapet rose wordlessly and, muttering an Armenian incantation to ward off evil spirits, plodded his weary way towards the bar. Life was a giant car wash, and he was on a bicycle.

Later, while downing his third slivovitz and holy water, he was joined by the Rabbit, followed by the Owl and the Penguin, who had come to kibitz the meeting of the two Children of Destiny.

"What possessed you to play the queen of spades on the second round?" bemoaned Karapet.

"I, er ... that is ... I'd rather not comment," mumbled the embarrassed Rabbit.

"Note the significance of the word 'possessed'!" whispered the Owl to the Penguin.

"Shush!" whispered the Penguin to the Owl.

"You owe me an explanation, R.R.," pleaded Karapet. "Put me out of my misery."

"Well, I don't want to offend you," blushed R.R. "But, you see, I was still hoping to get you down by ruffing a diamond, because—"

"But I was bound to draw trumps," argued the Free Armenian.

"That's what I thought," clamoured the excited Rabbit. "So I put up my queen to make you think it was my last trump. I know you are a fine player, and you never miscount, but there's always a first time, you see, and nobody is infallible. Why, even you forgot to take my queen with your king, which cost you the contract, so ... Anyway, I had this feeling that the queen was the right card to play, and it worked."

"Notice that he experienced an inexplicable feeling," murmured the Owl to the agnostic Penguin.

"He did not say it was inexplicable," retorted P.P.

"Well I do," stated O.O. "It's as plain as the nose on your face. If the Four Horsemen of the Apocalypse rode down the street, you'd insist that the Beauvoir Hunt had taken a wrong turning."

"Scepticism is the first step on the road to Philosophy," quoted the pompous Penguin.

"So I've heard," countered Oscar. "You took your own first step many years ago, P.P. And we're still waiting for your second."

Chapter 13

A New Ball Game

"It's a disgrace," complained Walter the Walrus to Timothy the Toucan.

"I'm inclined to agree with you," soothed the Toucan, who would have sided with Atilla the Hun or Vlad the Impaler. "But I expect the committee knows what it's doing."

"I admire your faith, Timothy," said Colin the Corgi. "But wasn't the camel the result of a committee's attempt to design a horse?"

As nobody seemed to know the answer, C.C. began to read aloud from the announcement on the club's notice board, for the benefit of the three rows of Griffins who were straining for a closer view.

Because of the phenomenally high standard of entries for the Millennium prizes, it has been officially decided that the task of judging them is beyond human ability. Since all the club's Superhumans are current contenders, the Committee has decided to change Rule 37, sub-sections 3.1 and 3.2, which will now read:

3.1   If two or more entries are considered to be of equal merit, the prize will be awarded to the player who submits the largest number of worthy entries during the period of the competition. These may be back dated to, but must on no account precede, the opening date of the competition.

3.2   No single entry will be accepted for more than three separate events.

"In other words, 'never mind the quality, feel the width'," jeered Papa. "Which means the Hog will scoop the pool. He will bombard them with every Bath coup and deep finesse he can muster. And he plays twice as many rubbers as anybody else, and five times as many contracts."

He glanced at the hall mirror to check the quality of his sneer, and made a dignified exit.

"There goes my chance of a brilliancy prize," grieved Walter. "I've only submitted one hand."

"I know the one," jibed Colin. "Your partner had miscounted his points and you made three no trumps on a combined count of only twenty-five."

Before the egregious Walrus could enumerate the signalling methods he had used to land the contract, the door of the card room flew open, and the club's Resident Cleaner swept out, signalling that it was open for business, and precipitating a stampede of members, anxious to lay claim to the weakest opponents.

True or False

It was late afternoon when the Hog appeared, fresh from two seven-course luncheons and exuding goodwill to all men. He even smiled when he cut Papa against the Corgi and the Walrus.

"Don't panic, Themistocles," he comforted his scowling partner. "You and I have been in tight corners before. We'll pull through if you sit back and let me play the contracts. And no false-carding, please. It doesn't bother me, but it causes you to miscount the hand. Ha! Ha! By the way, I'm told they've announced some new rules for the competition. I hope they spur you on to greater efforts."

Both sides had made an easy game when Walter dealt this hand:

Game All. Dealer North.

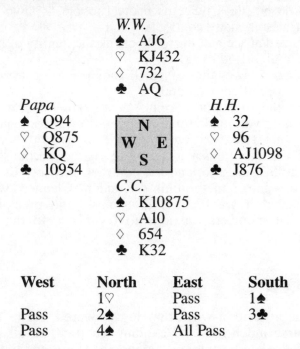

W.W.
♠ AJ6
♡ KJ432
◇ 732
♣ AQ

Papa
♠ Q94
♡ Q875
◇ KQ
♣ 10954

H.H.
♠ 32
♡ 96
◇ AJ1098
♣ J876

C.C.
♠ K10875
♡ A10
◇ 654
♣ K32

West	North	East	South
	1♡	Pass	1♠
Pass	2♠	Pass	3♣
Pass	4♠	All Pass	

Papa began with the ◇K and continued the suit. The Hog overtook the second round and returned the ◇10. This seemed the perfect setting for one of the Greek's vast repertoire of swindles. He ruffed his partner's winner and advanced the ♣10, looking for all the world like a man with no trump honour to protect. He would teach the Hog a lesson or die in the attempt.

The Corgi raised an inscrutable eyebrow, won on the table and cashed two top trumps, grinning when the ♠Q fell.

"You have saddened me, Themistocles." H.H. wagged a disappointed finger, as declarer wrapped up ten easy tricks. "You missed the chance to treat us to an unusual deceptive play."

"I treated you to the only deception available," claimed Papa. "It should be obvious even to you that as soon as declarer discovered I held only two diamonds, my queen of spades was dead. When I ruffed your winner it was …"

"It certainly was not," interrupted the Hog. "It might have

outwitted the younger residents of *The Little House on the Prairie*. Goldilocks might have used it to bamboozle the three bears. But your antique swindle would never fool one of my most promising pupils."

"Why, thank you, H.H." Colin's voice was thick with emotion. "I'm genuinely underwhelmed."

The Hog silenced him with a pedagogic glare, and turned superciliously to his partner. "Pretending you were in a hurry to lead through dummy's club tenace was like firing a pea-shooter at a Sherman tank. You could tell I didn't particularly want a club lead from my return at trick three. Listen carefully – I may ask questions later."

He began to enumerate the signalling options, while the Walrus nodded with awed reverence. "My lowest card would have requested a club, my knave would have demanded a heart, and my ten informed you that I was a floating voter. So you knew perfectly well that Colin held the king of clubs, and he knew that you knew."

"And surely you knew that I knew that you knew," added the Corgi helpfully.

"Of course I knew!" shouted Papa. "But finding you asleep was my only hope."

"You had a better one," argued the Hog. "You should have exploited your reputation by throwing a prosaic club on the third round of diamonds. Coming from you, that would have fooled anyone. Colin might well have ignored the percentages and played me for the trump queen. Why should he suspect you of true-carding? You even false-card when you play snap."

While the Hog adroitly purloined a whisky and soda from a tray which was en route to the Secretary Bird, a callow kibitzer, who, having completed the first stage of his apprenticeship, had earned the right to pose questions during the post-mortem, decided to exercise his privilege. As it was his maiden speech, it was preceded by a nervous twitch.

"May I ask …?" he began timidly.

"Of course you may," the Hog assured him. "Especially when the question is such an intelligent one. I can best answer it by a general comment on the noble art of hornswoggling. If Walter told us that he consistently told the truth, we should believe him unreservedly."

"I should certainly hope you would," announced the Walrus stiffly.

"Every card he plays tells a story," continued H.H. "And every story belongs firmly in the non-fiction shelves. To doubt him would be absurd. But should we believe the man who tells us he consistently lies? Of course not, for by admitting the fact, he has taken the first step on the rocky road to truth."

As the apprentice sat in open-mouthed admiration of this deeply flawed logic, the Hog cast an avuncular beam in the direction of Papa.

"If I may say so, Themistocles, it is time you took that first step. I know it will be a painful one, but the character of a consistent liar has passed its sell-by date."

While Papa sat, silently plotting revenge, the Hog raised his glass chivalrously. "But cheer up, I shall recommend your museum piece for one of those Gallant Failure awards. And may you have many more of them. Remember, it's quantity that counts, so let's feel the width."

Chapter 14

A Grudge Match

"The bane of duplicate," complained the Hideous Hog, not for the first time, "is that it makes for mediocre play."

Not noticing that Papa had entered the bar, he paused for effect, and the Greek took swift advantage of the loss of tempo.

"Yes, H.H., we've heard it so often we could all join in the chorus. It's pure Gilbert and Sullivan." He astounded his fellow Griffins by breaking into an embarrassingly tuneless chant:

> *"When a fellow knows another*
> *Holds the same cards that he holds,*
> *There's no thrill in making five from three and one,*
> *Three and one.*

Why, even you, slumming in a friendly match, made a small slam on a triple squeeze. And your achievement was in no way diminished by my overtrick in the other room."

"I remember it well," recalled the Hog. "You were so pleased with yourself, you forgot to tell us that the Rabbit revoked twice."

"Of course, there's something to be said for both forms," mediated Oscar. "To begin with ..."

"Exactly," agreed H.H. "What better place to begin than the Roaring Thirties, and those epic battles between Lenz and Culbertson, when every coup, gaffe and psyche was front page news. That was rubber bridge at its gladitorial best, the glory that was Rome." A look of disgust distorted his shiny pink countenance. "Can you imagine those plebs in the Colosseum, unable to cheer Spartacus until they knew what Tony Curtis had done in the Parthenon? Of course not. They would never have stood for it."

He surveyed the table for a loose drink, but every glass was under maximum security. Enfeebled by thirst, he seemed ready to wilt before Papa's counter-attack.

"Admit it, H.H. You only hate duplicate because there's no money in it. You might pocket the odd fee for helping a rich palooka pick up a few master points, but he might want to play the occasional contract."

The Greek's heavy-lidded eyes began to acquire a Mephistophelian glint. "You'd be the first to sing the praises of IMPs if the stakes were high enough ... and the odds were sufficiently tempting."

"Really?" purred H.H. "What degree of temptation had you in mind?"

Papa lit a gold-tipped cigarette and blew an intricate web of smoke rings. "It so happens that I have a European Champion spending a few days with me," he said in his silkiest voice. "Beppo Walenski, no less. I'm sure I could persuade him to play a few boards, provided you don't think you'd be overmatched."

"Not if I have the Rabbit and Beppo has you," rejoined the Hog equably.

"I will partner Karapet," insisted the Greek. "And to counterweight R.R. I'll ask Beppo to play with the Toucan. The quality of Timothy's dummy play will not be tested."

"And I'll take Colin the Corgi and the Secretary Bird," countered the Hog. "With S.B. in the other room, I won't have to set eyes on him until we score up. But let's discuss those tempting odds ..."

The trap was well and truly sprung. But the Owl couldn't for the life of him decide who had sprung it.

Madame Fortella

"Your astral charts are crystal clear," said Madame Fortella, the Rabbit's new multi-media medium. "And they are borne out by the tea leaves and the tarot cards. Your lucky suits will be hearts and spades."

"The majors," offered R.R. keenly.

"And even luckier will be – what is the expression? My friends from the Spirit World call it *sans à tout*."

"No trumps," he translated proudly. Then his face fell. "But he won't let me bid them!" he croaked.

Two cold dark eyes gleamed at him through dank layers of sinister mascara. "He?" she hissed. "And who is he who dares to defy the stars? Could it be that hideous one who will be your twin pole in this ..." She consulted her shorthand notes of the Rabbit's confused mumblings. "This battle of the century?"

"Yes," cringed R.R. "I'm only allowed to mention *sans à tout* when I'm going to be *le mort*."

With a cluck of disapproval, she slid a rune-filled parchment towards her timorous client. "Regard closely. On the night of the battle, no trumps will spell doom for the hideous one. Can you not see it?"

"I'm afraid not," confessed the Rabbit sadly. "I'm a complete fool at predicting the future. And I know I always will be."

Madame Fortella kept a straight face. Paradox always amused her, but smiling was bad for her image. "Then believe me," she exhorted. "Only clubs and diamonds will bring him *bon chance*."

"The minors," the Rabbit gurgled in fluent French. "But he only bids those when he hasn't got any."

"Courage, my rueful one. When he mentions the minors you must raise him fearlessly." She appraised him shrewdly, and decided he needed an escape clause. "Unless you prefer to bid *sans à tout*," she conceded handsomely.

When the Rabbit had departed, Madame Fortella slid his fat cheque into a slim leather case, and took out a complimentary ticket for a four week Mediterranean cruise. The pickings would be mouth-watering.

And she had been assured that the Papadopoulos Line was the last word in luxury.

Karapet's Pas de Deux

"It's an honour to play with you," fawned the Toucan. "Only I'm afraid I shall let you down badly."

"My friend," Beppo Walenski instructed him. "Do not say such things. When I was a youth in Schlemilograd, my father told me never to let a woman know I was not worthy of her. 'Let it come as a surprise', he said."

"But don't overdo it, Timothy," warned Papa. "Try not to surprise Beppo too much."

Victorious in the cut, Papa elected to play the first twelve boards against H.H. and the Rabbit.

Every inch of the Hog's fine figure radiated self-confidence, from the Burgundy tie, tastefully perfumed with the finest vintages, to the vast, convex corporation, proclaiming that its owner was a legend in his own lunchtime. Having been on a strict diet for nearly an hour, he was in peak physical condition.

Even the Rabbit seemed vaguely hopeful. He was the first to admit that the other three players were his superiors in certain aspects of the game – card play and bidding, for example, but these marginal differences were more than offset by his privileged glimpse into the future according to Mme Fortella.

The first few boards were uneventful. Both sides made contracts so foolproof that not even the most imaginative kibitzer could envisage a swing.

Then came the incredible board six.

East/West Game. Dealer West.

```
                    Papa
                    ♠ Q94
                    ♡ J653
                    ◇ A874
                    ♣ K2
     R.R.                              H.H.
     ♠ –              ┌─────────┐      ♠ 83
     ♡ AKQ8742        │   N     │      ♡ 109
     ◇ KQJ1032        │ W   E   │      ◇ –
     ♣ –              │   S     │      ♣ QJ10987653
                      └─────────┘
                    Karapet
                    ♠ AKJ107652
                    ♡ –
                    ◇ 965
                    ♣ A4
```

West	North	East	South
6♡	Dble	Pass	6♠
Pass	Pass	Dble	All Pass

Considering that most Griffins needed only a useful Yarborough to punish the Rabbit's slams, Papa's double was an underbid by several decibels, but he made up for it by his deafening roar when Karapet took out to six spades.

The Hog's double requested an unusual lead, but R.R., knowing that the majors were his lucky suits, stubbornly tabled the ♡A.

One glance at dummy convinced Karapet that he had made a phantom sacrifice. Then, when he visualised the Rabbit's thirteen red cards, he almost broke with five centuries of family tradition by smiling at the card table.

The Witch was at it again. The hand had the same theme as the classic he had misplayed a few days ago. Again, he must rectify the count for a red-suit squeeze but, given the chance, West would break up the squeeze, so a trick must be lost to East. But this time there were two chances of doing so.

He ruffed with a carefully chosen ♠5, and played the ♠J, overtaking with the queen. If the Hog played the ♠3, he would eliminate clubs and throw H.H. in with a spade. The forced ruff and discard would set the scene for the deadly squeeze against his partner.

But the Hog spoiled the first of declarer's chances by following with a far-sighted ♠8. Although Karapet began to feel the first pangs of doubt, he was ready with Plan B. After crossing to dummy's ♠Q to draw the last trump, he called for the ♣K. H.H., still one jump ahead, contributed the ♣5. Karapet, refusing to give up hope, completed his masterpiece by overtaking with the ace and firing out his two low clubs. Alas, he was forced to watch his opponent complete his act of vandalism by neatly inserting the ♣3.

It was not until declarer sadly conceded two diamond tricks that the kibitzers began to appreciate the quality of the play.

"Why does it always happen to me?" pleaded Karapet. "I salute you, H.H., but even if the Toucan had been in your seat, he would have sunk me by some unimaginable accident." He stared darkly into space. "Except that it would be no accident."

"In the other room, Colin is also likely to find the well-reasoned removal to six spades," laughed the Hog. "And Zippo, or whatever his name is, lacking my partner's, er, flair, will no doubt find a diamond lead. Two down, and a seven imp swing to your side. But what does the score matter? You have shared in a *pas de deux* worthy of Nijinsky and Nureyev at the peak of their partnership."

He gave his fellow artist's shoulder a congratulatory pat. "I'm so pleased you rejected the dull alternative of cashing the ace of clubs and all the trumps but one," he said, as he drew a five card ending:

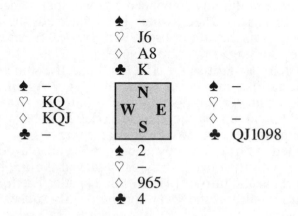

"Now you have set up a prosaic trump squeeze without the count. A club to the king will be too much even for such an accomplished escapologist as R.R. But I far prefer your artistic approach. Especially when I am your opponent," he chortled.

For most players, the Hog's analysis would have been a shattering blow, but Karapet merely shook his head sadly.

"Actually," observed Oscar, "six hearts cannot be defeated. And incidentally you three players must be favourites for the All Round Brilliancy Prize. Karapet's line, although flawed, was undeniably brilliant."

"What?" roared Papa. "Apart from Karapet overlooking that elementay coup, what about that fatuous opening lead?"

"From each according to his means," recited O.O. "R.R. played correctly to the subsequent twelve tricks. What more can we ask?"

"A *pas de trois*," murmured Sophia to the Rabbit, who was so delighted that he forgot to blame the Hog for throwing away an easy defensive trick.

Chapter 15

The Hog Takes the Lead

"Very flat boards so far," remarked the Secretary Bird, in an effort to be friendly to his famous opponent.

Beppo, on the theory that friendship had no place at the bridge table, replied with an ill-humoured grunt. Then, on the next deal, he was given the opportunity to show why he was one of the most feared players in Europe, especially by his partners.

Love All. Dealer South.

S.B.
- ♠ 964
- ♡ 109543
- ◇ 4
- ♣ Q1075

Beppo
- ♠ KJ532
- ♡ A
- ◇ J5
- ♣ AKJ64

T.T.
- ♠ Q107
- ♡ J7
- ◇ KQ862
- ♣ 832

C.C.
- ♠ A8
- ♡ KQ862
- ◇ A10973
- ♣ 9

West	North	East	South
			1♡
1♠	2♡	2♠	3◇
4♠	5♡	Dble	All Pass

S.B.'s uncharacteristic five heart bid was in the monster class, and Beppo was keen to inflict the maximum punishment. His match fee was sufficient to keep him in vodka for five years, and he intended to earn every kilolitre.

As his partner's double was presumably based on diamond values, a trump lead stood out a mile. When a glance at dummy confirmed the need to draw a second round, he pondered on the chances of giving his partner the lead. Finally, with a masterful air, he produced the ♠J.

The Toucan was not to be caught napping. He always covered his opponent's honours, never his partner's. When he played low, the Corgi ducked, and nothing could stop him cross-ruffing his way to ten tricks and escaping for a mere one down.

When Beppo realised that his expert defence had been sabotaged, he made sure it would not be forgotten.

"Why didn't you overtake my knave?" he berated Timothy. "Then declarer must capture."

"So he must," apologised the Toucan. "I'm afraid I'm not in your class."

"Class? What has class got to do with it? A kindergarten class would see that by playing the queen you tell me that you have the ten."

"Yes, of course I see that now," fawned the Toucan. "Was the ten important then?"

"Important?" sneered Beppo. "It only meant that I could safely underlead a spade to put you in for a trump lead. Two down instead of one. But perhaps to a player of your class two hundred points is not important. I congratulate you."

"You explain it beautifully," smooged T.T. "I'll know what to do next time."

He was so excited he forgot to bounce. He had been comprehensively disparaged by a world class player. It was better than becoming a Life Master. He suspected that Themistocles had paid Beppo a large fee. If so, he would offer to go halves.

Later, the Hog greeted the news of Beppo's fruitless masterplay with suitable derision. "Our European Champion forgot that the Griffins are not part of Europe," he said. "At our table, they reached the same asinine contract. I was West, the Rabbit having exercised his mystic right to change seats the moment Sirius came into conjunction with Betelgeuse Five."

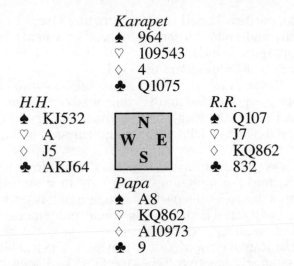

Karapet
♠ 964
♡ 109543
◇ 4
♣ Q1075

H.H.
♠ KJ532
♡ A
◇ J5
♣ AKJ64

R.R.
♠ Q107
♡ J7
◇ KQ862
♣ 832

Papa
♠ A8
♡ KQ862
◇ A10973
♣ 9

As H.H. paused to take a sip of Oscar's Armagnac, the Owl could see that he was about to bare his soul, and that no safety play was available.

"I admit it," confessed the Hog. "I too considered leading that jack of spades, but in the nick of time I remembered who was sitting opposite. I chose a small one, and R.R.'s queen drew Papa's ace. When I came in with a club, I led a low spade to his ten. The odds on his holding it were two to one, though I must admit I held my breath while I calculated the chances of the correct return. It isn't my habit to show emotion at the table, but you must remember I had been fasting for two hours."

He thrust a breadstick reflectively into his smoked salmon dip, and took a restorative bite.

"When the Rabbit produced that trump, I thanked his lucky stars. It never ceases to amaze me that even the most clueless players can occasionally do the right thing. But only if you are kind to them – not by buttering them up, but by making life easy for them. Zippo's expert lead was unforgivably cruel to the Toucan. I hope he made up for it in the post-mortem."

The G.A.'s Quintuple Coup

"Well done, partner," cried the Hog, causing Oscar to choke on his Campari and soda. "I cannot remember when I last heard such fine, pragmatic bidding."

"Neither can I," shuddered the Owl.

Board eleven had provided the Rabbit with his first opportunity to apply Madame Fortella's advice. After opening 2NT, he had raised the Hog's 3♣ Stayman enquiry to five. H.H duly collected eleven tricks with several finesses and a *coup en passant*.

"R.R. was quite right to bypass the laydown three no trumps," he told the kibitzers. "With only nine sure tricks, he knew it was safer to let his partner struggle in a twenty per cent alternative contract. Thanks to his sound judgement, we were able to avoid an adverse swing."

While the Rabbit glowed, Oscar frowned. The Rabbit's Angel had been strangely inactive. True, the G.A. had been labouring under two restrictions: the boards had been pre-dealt and sorted; and there would be no cherry-brandy-and-biscuits break until the halfway stage.

Then, as the Rabbit picked up his hand for board twelve, the G.A. gave a display of virtuosity calculated to turn even the sceptical Penguin into a believer.

A young, perspiring kibitzer decided to risk the Owl's wrath by opening a door without written permission.

The rush of cold air exacted a cyclonic sneeze from the Rabbit, whose cards fell to the floor.

Against odds of 2^{13} to 1, they all landed face downwards.

Finally, when he sorted them with trembling fingers, he placed the ♣3 with his spades.

Four down and one to go:

North/South Game. Dealer West.

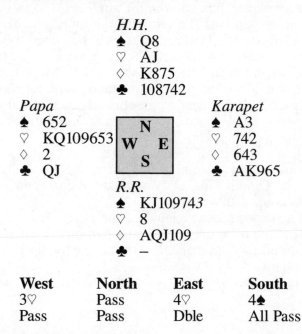

H.H.
♠ Q8
♡ AJ
◊ K875
♣ 108742

Papa
♠ 652
♡ KQ109653
◊ 2
♣ QJ

Karapet
♠ A3
♡ 742
◊ 643
♣ AK965

R.R.
♠ KJ109743
♡ 8
◊ AQJ109
♣ —

West	North	East	South
3♡	Pass	4♡	4♠
Pass	Pass	Dble	All Pass

Karapet bid on the popular assumption that nobody went broke through doubling the Rabbit. Papa led the ◊2. Even R.R. had a vague suspicion that this was a singleton, but seeing no way of going down, he decided to indulge his congenital fondness for ruffing. He took the first trick in hand, crossed to the ♡A, and trumped the knave with what he believed was the three of spades.

It was not until Papa claimed the trick and continued with a club that R.R. identified his error, but before he could stammer his excuses, a guffaw from the Hog told him that he had done something inexplicably clever. He smiled shyly at Sophia, and proceeded to make ten easy tricks.

"You've done it again," snarled Papa. "If you fell into a beehive, you would emerge unscathed, clutching a honeycomb labelled 'with love from the queen'. Had you played like a normal palooka we would have made two aces and two diamond ruffs."

"But it just so happens that I'm not a normal palooka,"

squeaked the Rabbit defiantly. "I'm an abnormal pal– er, I mean I'm a better player than you think I am."

"Of course you are." The Hog leapt gallantly to his partner's defence. "It seems that to lesser players," he leered insultingly at Papa, "your scissors coup, removing Karapet's entry for the second diamond ruff, was a masterstroke. To you, partner, I realise it was a routine precaution, taken without thought and without malice. By sparing yourself such unnecessary cerebral activity, you are able to save your brain for more important tasks, such as not revoking. Ha! Ha!"

"I still say he is a ..." insisted Papa.

"You are wrong to blame R.R.," intoned Karapet. "Blame the curse of the Djoulikyans. Only against me can declarer execute a scissors coup with a ruff."

"And a suicide sneeze," laughed the Hog.

Ignoring the interruption, Papa turned on his partner. "If you were so sure he would make the contract, why did you double?" he challenged.

"Because I never learn," sobbed Karapet. "It's part of the curse."

Chapter 16

A Melodramatic Rescue

"Would you care to raise the stakes?" asked the Hideous Hog, after agreeing the half-time score with Papa.

"How sporting of you," purred Papa. "Could the fact that you are now in the lead have anything to do with your generous suggestion?"

While waving his hand in a gesture of dismissal, the Hog contrived to seize the last two *fois gras* sandwiches.

"I've left the fish paste and watercress," he said. "I know they're your favourites." Seeing that Papa's glass was empty, he reluctantly drank from his own. "And what is twelve imps? A mere bagatelle. Remember, Themistocles, you are the best player in the club – I hope I'm quoting you correctly. And with an international superstar in support, surely you are not afraid to add a modest case of *Krug* to the side bets?"

"Not in the least." Papa rose to the bait, and smartly sprang a trap of his own. "Let's make it an immodest two cases. The winner to choose the vintage."

"Agreed," leered the Hog, managing to appear more sanguine than he felt. Sotheby's were holding a champagne auction next week, and two dozen of one of the great years could cost at least a fortnight's winnings.

He would have been even less confident had he known how the Rabbit was going to bid board thirteen. At Papa's table the auction was textbook, while Karapet's play was anything but.

Game All. Dealer South.

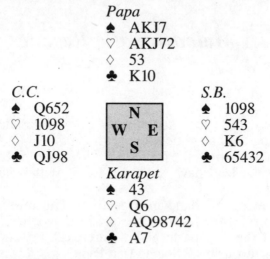

Papa
♠ AKJ7
♡ AKJ72
♢ 53
♣ K10

C.C.
♠ Q652
♡ 1098
♢ J10
♣ QJ98

S.B.
♠ 1098
♡ 543
♢ K6
♣ 65432

Karapet
♠ 43
♡ Q6
♢ AQ98742
♣ A7

South	West	North	East
1♢	Pass	1♡	Pass
2♢	Pass	2♠	Pass
3♢	Pass	4♢	Pass
5♣	Pass	6♢	All Pass

The Corgi led the ♣Q, and Karapet could see that only an adverse trump break could endanger the contract. As a sound technician, he was familiar with the standard safety play of laying down the ace, but he didn't regard it as a bosom friend. To the Free Armenian, a safety play should cater not for a bad break, but a natural disaster.

After winning the first trick in dummy, he catered for a four-nil trump break by finessing the ♢7. When it lost to Colin's ten, he won the club return, crossed to the table with a spade, and called for dummy's last trump. If the knave appeared on his right, he intended to finesse with a degree of confidence amounting to certainty.

When the ♢K landed on the table, he spread his hand with a woebegone expression. What was that cursed witch up to? The answer came to him in a blinding flash. She was lurking in the other room, waiting to chivvy his opponents into the laydown grand slam.

"I admire the way you handled trumps," acclaimed the Corgi. "What it lacked in correctness, it made up for in originality."

"They had no right to break two-two," explained Karapet. "When a Djoulikyan is declarer, four-nil is the norm. If the Professor had held four, you would have been applauding my foresight."

"Hardly applauding," contradicted Colin. "Perhaps lost in rapt admiration."

When the board arrived at the other table, Beppo Walenski was deep in conversation with Sophia the Siren, much to the consternation of the Rabbit, who failed to hear his partner's opening one diamond bid. With his swarthy good looks, the European Champion reminded him of the villain in a Victorian melodrama, bent on subjecting the heroine to a fate worse than death.

Even though he had no idea of what that fate was, he was about to leap to her rescue, when Beppo picked up the Hog's convention card, stared in disbelief at the illegible wine-stained scribblings, and flung it down in disgust.

"What is the strength of your no trump?" he demanded.

"Weak," explained H.H., in the loud measured tones he always used when talking to dogs and foreigners. "Twelve to fourteen points."

It was hardly surprising that the Rabbit proceeded to bid on the premise that his partner had opened one no trump.

In theory, Beppo's double requested a diamond lead. In practice, having been informed of R.R.'s unique prowess, he was doubling on principle. The Rabbit's redouble was S.O.S., but was passed by the Hog, who pictured him with a powerful two-suiter.

Apart from these trifling misunderstandings, the auction was uneventful.

(hand rotated for convenience)

H.H.
♠ 43
♡ Q6
◇ AQ98742
♣ A7

T.T.
♠ 1098
♡ 543
◇ K6
♣ 65432

Beppo
♠ Q652
♡ 1098
◇ J10
♣ QJ98

R.R.
♠ AKJ7
♡ AKJ72
◇ 53
♣ K10

South	West	North	East
		1◇	Pass
2♣	Pass	2◇	Pass
3♡	Pass	4◇	Pass
4♠	Pass	6♣	Dble
Rdble	All Pass		

When his redouble was passed out, R.R.'s strangulated gulp, and the subsequent oscillation of his Adam's apple, were audible throughout the club. He was sure of two things: the Hog had erred grievously, but he, the Rabbit, would be blamed.

The Toucan proudly led his small diamond, and the Rabbit contemplated the horrifying spectacle of the Hog's dummy.

"But H.H. ..." he retaliated.

"Just do your best, partner," the Hog consoled him. "But don't do anything dangerous, such as thinking."

Knowing from long experience that, when skating on thin ice, speed was the only hope, R.R. rattled off eight side-suit winners, successfully finessing in diamonds and spades. To do him justice, he had no intention of making the contract; he was simply following his usual policy of trying to go down by as few tricks as possible.

When he finally paused for breath, this was the five-card ending, with the lead, quite fortuitously, in declarer's hand:

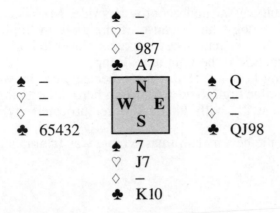

```
              ♠  —
              ♡  —
              ◇  987
              ♣  A7
♠  —                        ♠  Q
♡  —          N             ♡  —
◇  —        W   E           ◇  —
♣  65432       S            ♣  QJ98
              ♠  7
              ♡  J7
              ◇  —
              ♣  K10
```

At this point, more in anger than hope, he advanced his last spade. When the Toucan ruffed, R.R. had sufficient faith in his best friend to place him with five trumps. Could Beppo also have five? It seemed unlikely, but, bearing in mind the man was a European Champion, not impossible.

Suddenly, he miraculously remembered that the spade finesse had succeeded, and Beppo still had the queen. With a squeak of triumph, he ruffed with the ♣7, and called for a diamond. He overruffed Beppo's ♣Q with the ♣K, ruffed a heart with dummy's ♣A, and Beppo could not stop him making his club ten with a *coup en passant*. For the first time in his eventful life R.R. had made a slam without rectifying the count until trick thirteen.

Every sagging centimetre of Beppo Walenski's lithe body proclaimed that he was a beaten man. His career was studded with victories against most of the world's great players, but none of them had prepared him for a phenomenon like the Rabbit. Realising that the situation called for some sort of comment, he opened his mouth, but, to his horror, no sound would emerge.

"Genius is the word you are looking for, my dear Zippo," chortled H.H. "My partner scorned the easy diamond slam, because he knew it wouldn't be doubled. Admittedly he took a risk, but, in view of the quality of his dummy play, it was quite justified. Now that you have seen his mettle, you'll know better than to double him in the future. But for your, shall we say, unfortunate intervention, Timothy would undoubtedly have led a trump, and you would have been sixteen imps in instead of ten out."

The Rabbit was incandescent with pride. Not because of the Hog's ironic eulogy, but because of the glow in Sophia's eyes, and the fact that she had edged her chair closer to him, and away from the clutches of the villainous Beppo.

Wondering how to acknowledge her gesture, he was seized by an irresistible urge to do something heroic. Gripping the seat of his chair with both hands, he reciprocated by nearly a millimetre!

As in all the best melodramas, virtue was triumphant.

Chapter 17

Swings and Roundabouts

"The Hog is worried," whispered Oscar.

"He looks supremely confident," protested the Penguin.

"But he has gone nearly twenty minutes without insulting his partner," explained the Owl.

The three preceding boards had been catastrophes. Beppo landed a slam which depended on a hair-raising finesse, two suits breaking three-three and an ingenious misdefence by the Rabbit. Next, R.R., slyly concealing his three-card support for partner's six-card major, went down in a no trump game. Finally, holding two red doubletons opposite a red two-suiter, R.R. passed the Hog's four diamond bid, considerately leaving him to make ten tricks in his lucky suit, rather than the same number in the unlucky major.

Instead of subjecting his partner to the mandatory verbal assault, H.H. took the humane and unprecedented step of taking him to one side.

"R.R.," counselled the Hog, "it is obvious that your flair has deserted you. If and when you regain your talent for inspired lunacy, I shall again honour you with the friendly abuse that you know and love. In the meantime, something is seriously wrong, and I intend to find out what it is."

"Well, you see, er ... I don't know quite how to tell you this, H.H., bbbut ..." stammered the Rabbit. "But I went to see this medium. She was highly recommended ..."

As the Hog absorbed the account of the mysterious medium's astrological bidding system, he unerringly deduced that its source lay not in the stars, but in the fertile brain of a certain conniving ship-owner.

"That Greek shall pay dearly for this," he prophesied.

"Oh, I don't think she's Greek," speculated the Rabbit. "She speaks French with a Spanish accent, and looks Italian, or perhaps Portuguese."

"Never mind," soothed the Hog. "But having seen a lead of twenty-odd imps turn into a substantial deficit, I suggest we replace the Fortella system with our own inimitable version of Acol. So from now on you must support my majors with powerful singletons, bid no trumps only in a dire emergency, and ..."

The Hog Fights Back

H.H. led the reprogrammed Rabbit back into the arena and greeted his opponents with a lupine grin which caused the Toucan to quake in his patent leather shoes and Beppo to long wistfully for the non-competitive atmosphere of a World Championship final.

Love All. Dealer West.

```
                        T.T.
                        ♠ A105
                        ♡ AK852
                        ◊ 543
                        ♣ A8
        R.R.                            H.H.
        ♠ KQJ632        ┌─────────┐     ♠ 7
        ♡ Q63           │    N    │     ♡ 1097
        ◊ Q2            │  W   E  │     ◊ K109876
        ♣ 72            │    S    │     ♣ 654
                        └─────────┘
                        Beppo
                        ♠ 984
                        ♡ J4
                        ◊ AJ
                        ♣ KQJ1093
```

South	West	North	East
	1♠	Dble	Pass
2♠	Pass	3♡	Pass
4♣	Pass	5♣	All Pass

Some poor bidding by the Toucan lured Beppo into a difficult five club contract, instead of the laydown three no trumps.

"You *tlikszhitchnik!*" cried the European Champion when he saw the dummy, and the Toucan, who, to the best of his recollection, had never been called a *tlikszhitchnik* before, bounced blissfully.

After West led the ♠K, declarer's chances of establishing the hearts seemed slim, until the vigilant superstar spotted an unusual line. Hoping to find East with three clubs and a singleton spade, not to mention a three-three heart break, he ducked the opening lead, expecting East to ruff the spade continuation. Now, as the cards lay, there would be eleven top tricks.

However, on the second round of spades, the Hog, with an infuriating grin, threw the ◇10. A lesser man than Beppo Walenski might have given up, but he immediately drew trumps, and considered how to duck a heart to East. Technically, the knave was the correct choice, hoping to find H.H. with ♡Qxx, but in view of West's opening bid and the Hog's high diamond discard, the queen was surely with that improbable Rabbit.

So Beppo, trusting with good reason to catch the rueful one off guard, led a low heart. The Rabbit has no idea why he rose with the ♡Q. He had a vague memory of sensing declarer's overwhelming confidence, concluding that something desperate was needed, and selecting the queen as the most desperate card available. Oscar the Owl's theory is that the G.A., ashamed of deserting his protégé during the Fortella period, was making amends.

Again, Beppo refused to admit defeat. After crossing to the ◇A, he ran the trump suit. This was the position when the last trump was led:

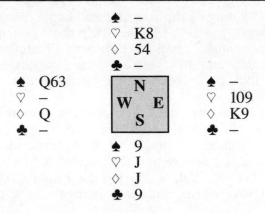

On the final trump, the Rabbit relinquished a spade, dummy threw a diamond, and the Hog had a problem so testing that it took him almost half a second of deep thought. If he pitched a small diamond, the Great Zippo Walenski would cash the ♡J, and throw him in with a diamond. Dummy's ♡K would now take the last trick.

So the Hog threw his ◇K, and Beppo was one down. Noticing his forlorn expression, H.H. decided to cheer him up.

"Bad luck, Zippo," he chortled. "You did your best, and if someone like Chemla had been in my seat no doubt you would have succeeded. I wish for your sake he had been."

The Final Board

Neither Chemla nor the Hog could have gained a significant advantage from any of the deals which followed, until the arrival of the sensational board twenty-four.

Beppo guessed that he was around fifteen IMPs ahead, although with such wild players it was impossible to be sure about anything.

"Leave everything to me," he whispered to the compliant Toucan, and nearly ate his words when he picked up a hand with a single high card point.

"Of course," the Toucan whispered back, while secretly praying for a flat Yarborough.

North/South Game. Dealer North.

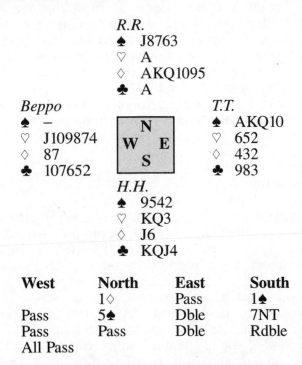

R.R.
♠ J8763
♡ A
◇ AKQ1095
♣ A

Beppo
♠ —
♡ J109874
◇ 87
♣ 107652

T.T.
♠ AKQ10
♡ 652
◇ 432
♣ 983

H.H.
♠ 9542
♡ KQ3
◇ J6
♣ KQJ4

West	North	East	South
	1◇	Pass	1♠
Pass	5♠	Dble	7NT
Pass	Pass	Dble	Rdble
All Pass			

As the Hog sorted his cards, he exuded the panache of a man with a sixty-IMP lead, and every intention of increasing it. Inwardly, he had no doubt that only a huge swing could save him from an unthinkable defeat.

His chances seemed remote, until the Toucan's emotional reaction to the Rabbit's unusually intelligent five spade bid. Among the clues to his powerful spade holding were three bounces of astonishment, an incredulous review of the bidding, and the note of sympathy in his voice as apologetically doubled his dearest friend. Later, H.H. described it as the finest example of table absence he had seen; the only improvement he could suggest was that Timothy might have enquired whether a defender could claim a hundred honours.

Hoping, with good reason, that Beppo was void in spades, the Hog immediately decided to remove to no trumps. But how many? Never one for half measures, he leapt to seven!

In the rational atmosphere of bridge at the summit, Beppo Walenski might well have deduced from the auction that a diamond lead might disrupt declarer's communications. But thinking rationally with the Rabbit and the Toucan at the table was like trying to compose a symphony in the Tower of Babel. When he chose to lead the ♡J, the Hog gloatingly collected thirteen highly immoral tricks.

At the other table, Papa had languished in five spades, which the cunning Corgi had refrained from doubling.

The Hog's team had triumphed by a whisker.

The Reckoning

Beppo was in deep shock. In his day he had seen off most of the world's best. He had hammered Helgemo, murdered Meckwell, chastened Chemla, and made life jolly difficult for Forrester. And now he had been humbled by the Hog and routed by the Rabbit.

Papa was relatively shockproof. But he was certainly not piqueproof. "I've never known such unbelievable luck," he grumbled, as he agreed the final score with the Hog.

"How kind of you to admit it," smirked H.H. "But I managed to scrape home in spite of it. And I've a feeling I'll be unlucky again when I visit Sotheby's. Their top vintage has a reserve price of only £200 a bottle."

"Make sure you get a receipt," snapped Papa.

"Naturally," gloated the Hog. "And make sure you get one from Madame Fortella."

"Who?" gasped Papa palely.

"Your private bridge tutor," H.H. reminded him. "Her advice was a little too advanced for R.R., but I can see what she has done for you, Themistocles. I've always wondered where you acquired your somewhat eccentric talents, and now I know. Ha! Ha!"

Chapter 18

Crime and Punishment

"I'm afraid we're out of the '87," apologised the Owl.

"Don't worry," his guest assured him. "I prefer the '98."

Oscar had chosen a quiet corner of the bar for Sophia the Siren's first tutorial. As she gazed at him over the rim of her champagne glass, her luminous eyes glowing with approbation, he felt that his investment in a bottle of *Dom Perignon* would be worth every penny, even though the dividend would be purely spiritual.

"In approximately one minute – I can't be more specific than that," he prophesied, "somebody will arrive at our table, bearing a used envelope, a sheet from a diary or, in the case of the Hog, a final demand for payment of his student loan. It will contain four hands, perhaps two, occasionally only one. But you may wager your last farthing that he has one of two purposes: to crow over a triumph, or to seek sympathy for having done the right thing with the wrong result. That is why he needs the services of a qualified and sensitive kibitzer. If he shows the deal to his rivals, they will seize every opportunity to be cleverer than he is."

"But surely, O.O., you are cleverer than all of them," gushed Sophia.

"Most of them," temporised the Owl. "And there are times when I am sorely tempted to prove it. But I didn't get where I am today without knowing when to say 'Get behind me, Satan'. You'll soon see what I mean – here comes our first patient."

It was Colin the Corgi, carrying an empty glass and a used envelope, both of which he placed without ceremony between Sophia and Oscar, while the battle-hardened Owl, without malice, placed the champagne bucket out of C.C.'s reach. The envelope contained the following diagram:

East/West Game. Dealer South.

Anon. Griffin
♠ 10976
♡ AKQ65
◊ Q5
♣ Q4

```
    N
 W     E
    S
```

C.C.
♠ AKJ85
♡ 7
◊ AJ84
♣ A76

South	West	North	East
1♠	Pass	2♡	Pass
3◊	Pass	3♠	Pass
4♣	Pass	5♠	Pass
6♠	Dble	All Pass	

"With supreme confidence in the quality of your dummy play," declared C.C., "you reach a spade slam which, in view of West's double, presents a stimulating challenge. The jack of hearts is led."

"Who are the other players?" enquired Oscar, in deference to the First Rule.

"May I tell you later?" procrastinated the Corgi. "Approach the problem like the fine academician you are."

After moving the champagne even further away from the Hog-trained Corgi, Oscar studied the deal, and saw a heaven sent opportunity to blood his pupil.

"Perhaps Sophia ...," he speculated.

"May I assume that you made the contract?" asked S.S., observing Rule Two and basking in Oscar's hoot of approval.

"Assume anything you wish," hedged Colin.

"Then I will deduce that the anonymous West holds the guarded queen of spades and both minor suit kings, and badly needs to read S.J. Simon on the mathematics of doubling."

"So it seems," grinned the Corgi. "In the meantime his education is in your fair hands."

"Then let's set the stage for a possible end play, Colin," recommended S.S. "I will take two top hearts, pitching a diamond, and ruff a third round. Does everyone follow?"

"Fortunately," said C.C. "But what they followed with won't help you. There were no Walruses at the table."

"So I will cash my two top trumps," stated Sophia. "If East shows out, as I expect, I will throw West in with a third. I need West to have no more hearts, and whichever minor suit he returns will give me two tricks and a ruff. My other losers go on dummy's heart winners."

"Reasoned like a master," approved C.C. "This is the distribution you so shrewdly envisaged. It's nice to know I am in such good company."

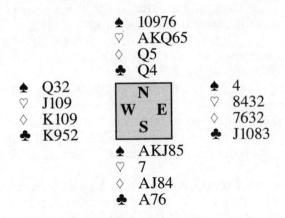

```
              ♠ 10976
              ♡ AKQ65
              ◇ Q5
              ♣ Q4
♠ Q32                        ♠ 4
♡ J109        N              ♡ 8432
◇ K109      W   E            ◇ 7632
♣ K952        S              ♣ J1083
              ♠ AKJ85
              ♡ 7
              ◇ AJ84
              ♣ A76
```

"Why, thank you, Colin," responded Sophia warmly. "And I hope that you thanked West for his generous double."

"I'm afraid West was our black sheep, Charlie the Chimp. After yawning ostentatiously throughout the auction, he leapt to life with a loud double which had all the classic overtones of confidence, avarice and triumph. It should surely win him the Chicanery award."

"You don't mean ..." began Oscar.

"Exactly." The Corgi jotted down two more hands. "I lied about the East and West holdings. They were very different."

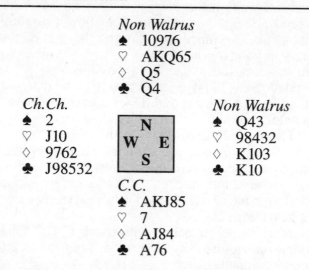

Non Walrus
♠ 10976
♡ AKQ65
◇ Q5
♣ Q4

Ch.Ch.
♠ 2
♡ J10
◇ 9762
♣ J98532

Non Walrus
♠ Q43
♡ 98432
◇ K103
♣ K10

C.C.
♠ AKJ85
♡ 7
◇ AJ84
♣ A76

"Charlie didn't actually follow to the third round of hearts, but by that stage it was too late to do anthing about it."

"I see," sighed Oscar. "Well it seems that Charlie took you in as surely as you took us in. Do you think it's a matter for the Laws and Ethics Committee?"

"Not really," replied the Corgi. "By the Chimp's standards, a double which registers on the Richter scale is merely a slight overbid. He also contrived to look like a man running for cover while I was preparing for my putative endplay. But he claimed he was still thinking about the hand before last. A cast-iron alibi."

"Nevertheless, I shall have a word with him," promised Oscar in a tone which would have made a braver man than the Chimp quake in his boots. "I take it that without his nefarious double you would have made the contract?"

"Diamond finesse at trick two, two rounds of trumps, ruff a diamond on the table, pitch my long clubs on winning hearts, cross to my ace of clubs, ruff my last diamond. No, Oscar, I wouldn't make it in a month of Sundays."

When Colin strutted off to seek another victim, Oscar poured some more *Dom Perignon*. "Your performance was flawless," he praised Sophia. "How did you guess that such a self-sufficient man wanted sympathy?"

"It's all in the eyes," she explained. "When I looked into his,

I knew he was afraid I might succeed where he failed. It was obvious that expert play had come unstuck, so I took the humane decision to be as unlucky as he was. I think on the whole it worked."

"Very clever," acknowledged the Owl, regarding her with heightened respect. Her progress had been more rapid than he had dared to hope. The day could not be far off when she would be addressed by her initials.

"Besides," she added archly. "The Hog had been dummy. He told me all about the deal an hour ago."

A Floored Defence

"A curious case," observed O.O. to his brothers-in-law on the Laws and Ethics Committee. "It actually involves a complaint against a kibitzer."

"Surely not," frowned an aged Griffin. "If it's upheld we'll never live it down. Who is the plaintiff?"

"I'm afraid he's the Emeritus Professor of Bio-Sophistry," replied Oscar. "So there's no chance of hushing it up."

"Then you'd better tell us the worst, young man," sighed an even more aged Griffin. "Afterwards, we can consider the best way to keep it out of those wretched tabloids."

"Oh, I don't think it will come to that," the Owl assured him.

"I never leave anything to chance," the even more ancient Griffin assured him. "Every morning when I wake, I read the *Times* obituary column. And I never get up until I've made sure I'm not in it."

This was the deal O.O. presented, with considerable diffidence:

Game All. Dealer North.

C.C.
♠ KJ10
♡ A1086
♢ AK973
♣ A

R.R.   D.D.

```
      N
   W     E
      S
```

S.B.
♠ A763
♡ QJ975
♢ 42
♣ Q8

South	West	North	East
		1♢	Pass
1♡	Pass	4♣	Pass
4♠	Pass	6♡	All Pass

The Rabbit led the ♣J. The Secretary Bird quite reasonably elected to test diamonds before touching trumps, since he would then know the best way to tackle the majors. He ruffed the third round with the ♡Q, and R.R. calmly discarded a spade. Relaxing visibly, S.B. stretched his long, spindly legs, a sure sign that his long, scholarly nose scented victory.

He ruffed his remaining club and another diamond, R.R. parting with a club. The prospect of finding East with a singleton or doubleton trump was excellent, in which case he would not have to find the spade queen. However, when he tried a trump to the ace, Dolly the Dove discarded with a soft murmur of apology which did nothing to soften declarer's heart.

He shot a virulent glance at the Rabbit, wondering how on earth such a scatterbrain could find such a defence.

This was the complete deal:

C.C.
♠ KJ10
♡ A1086
◇ AK973
♣ A

R.R.
♠ 52
♡ K432
◇ 65
♣ J10965

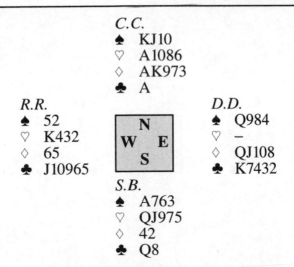

D.D.
♠ Q984
♡ –
◇ QJ108
♣ K7432

S.B.
♠ A763
♡ QJ975
◇ 42
♣ Q8

It was not until Dolly showed out that Sophia appeared to notice something near the Rabbit's feet.

"There seems to be a card on the floor," she observed.

After a hasty recount (totally unnecessary with R.R. at the table) Dolly, with a sigh of relief, announced that she had six.

"By a strange coincidence, so has dummy and so have I," threatened the Secretary Bird, his pince-nez gleaming accusingly at the Rabbit.

The defendant's blush almost reached the fingers he extended to accept the card, and he reddened further when he saw it was the ♡K.

"You realise the penalty for an exposed card," warned S.B., licking his thin lips at the thought of imposing a draconian sentence.

"Oh, but it wasn't exposed," smiled Sophia serenely. "It had landed face down and I made sure it stayed that way."

"There is a widely held view that kibitzers should be seen and not heard," asseverated S.B. "But I do not subscribe to it. Why should they be seen?"

Hissing in fluent Sanskrit, he addressed himself to a task normally performed by his left hand opponent – going down as few as possible.

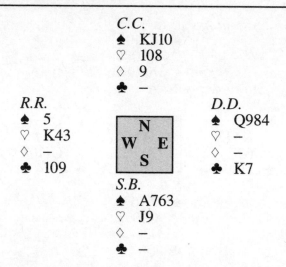

C.C.
♠ KJ10
♡ 108
◇ 9
♣ —

R.R.
♠ 5
♡ K43
◇ —
♣ 109

D.D.
♠ Q984
♡ —
◇ —
♣ K7

S.B.
♠ A763
♡ J9
◇ —
♣ —

Desperately, the Secretary Bird abandoned trumps. He called for dummy's master diamond, which was duly ruffed. Now, with his clubs providing safe exit cards, R.R. couldn't help making two more trumps to defeat the slam by two tricks.

"You haven't heard the last of this," promised S.B.

"See you in court," smiled S.S., winning the battle of clichés by a narrow margin.

The Professor's learned written submission concluded with a summary in lay terms.

Caveat Spectatur

1.   Without S.S.'s intervention, the Rabbit might have revoked.

2.   The timing of her fortuitous discovery of the missing card was suspicious on two counts.

2.1.   She had previously shown herself to be more than a competent kibitzer.

2.2   During previous post-mortems, she had frequently given the Rabbit support, which, though not illicit, was both partisan and inappropriate.

3.   Although the Defence might contend that, with two small hearts, the Rabbit would be unlikely to revoke (at least in that suit) his record clearly demonstrated his capacity to do so.

3.1.   The presence of the ♡K might actually have increased the possibility of a revoke.
(see Appendix I)

4.   While the contract might have failed even without the temporary absence of the ♡K, this can have no bearing on the decision of the court. If a burglar breaks open your safe, the fact that it happens to be empty is not a mitigating factor.

The Committee ruled that Sophia had acted with youthful impetuosity, but without malice. Her kibitzer's rights remained intact, and she was not required to compensate North/South for their lost slam or their alleged extra undertrick.

However, the Committee showed its teeth by sternly reiterating an earlier pronouncement.

If the players want to play with only 51 cards, they must be allowed to do so without interference.

Moreover, in a frank, no-nonsence interview, Oscar sternly informed Sophia that her career had been set back by several hours.

When the Hideous Hog was told of the outcome, he chortled gleefully.

"If ever that Secretary Bird is run over outside the Club," he predicted, "we'll know whose body it is without bothering to look." He paused for emphasis and a hearty swig of Oscar's *Chateau Latour.* "There will be no skid marks."

Chapter 19

A Lesson for the Toucan

While acknowledging that the Rueful Rabbit misunderstood more conventions than anyone in the Western Hemisphere, several good judges had observed that, as a result of R.R.'s expert tuition, Timothy the Toucan was becoming a dangerous contender. Every week the normally docile Rabbit persuaded his ever-willing pupil to add three new gadgets to their already awesome armoury.

"I know it's a lot to remember, Timothy," sympathised R.R., during one of their learned system discussions. "But the Hog says our bidding confuses all our opponents except him, because he never listens to it, and it doesn't matter that it confuses us, because we're at our best when we're confused, and it makes sense to play to our strengths. I'm not quite sure what he meant, but I think it was a compliment, and a compliment from H.H. has to be taken seriously."

"Very true." The Toucan put down his glass of Burgundy so that he could bounce enthusiastically in his seat. "What about playing the Polish strong pass?"

"I'm afraid it's not licensed," lamented the Rabbit. "And the Hog said that it wouldn't suit our style anyway, because we're both such good card holders that we would never be able to bid, although that might not be a bad thing. So this week I thought we could make do with two new conventions and sharpen up our signalling."

Panting heavily, he produced a bulky autographed manuscript of the Distinguished Bridge Author's most famous unpublished work, *Precision Signalling*, and proudly opened it at page 287.

"I think we ought to give up low discouraging, high encouraging," announced R.R. eruditely.

"Splendid," smiled T.T. "I'm not sure what it means, but I have an idea that I've never liked it."

"What would you like to play instead?" invited the Rabbit.

"What have you got?"

The Rabbit regarded his friend with affection. T.T. meant well, but he lacked the sharpness of intellect needed to cope with the advanced methods R.R. would have recommended to a fellow master. "I think we ought to do it the other way round," he said.

"Are you sure that's licensed?" Timothy looked shocked.

"I'm certain of it, but I'll check with Oscar," the Rabbit assured him. "And there must be a lot of advantages in playing HDLE, because it seems that, er ... well, anyway, it takes sixteen pages to explain them."

"I'll take your word for it," smiled the Toucan. "HLED it is."

"No, Timothy," explained R.R. patiently. It's High Discouraging, Low Encouraging."

"Even better," rejoiced T.T., and shook his head at the barman to signal that they were ready for another drink.

A Prize for Papa

That was the background to two deals which were to clinch a well-deserved Gallant Failure award for Papa, and to enhance the already fabulous reputation of the Rabbit. Needless to say, neither Papa nor Karapet had prepared any defence to the new secret weapon.

Love All. Dealer West.

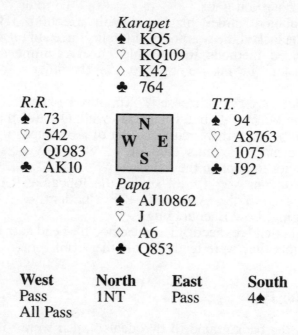

Karapet
♠ KQ5
♡ KQ109
◇ K42
♣ 764

R.R.
♠ 73
♡ 542
◇ QJ983
♣ AK10

T.T.
♠ 94
♡ A8763
◇ 1075
♣ J92

Papa
♠ AJ10862
♡ J
◇ A6
♣ Q853

West	North	East	South
Pass	1NT	Pass	4♠
All Pass			

After leading the ♣A, the Rabbit experienced a thrill of pride when his pupil followed with the ♣J. Confident that their new signalling methods were working like a well-oiled machine, he switched to the ◇Q, noting his partner's ◇10.

From the viewpoint of a callow young kibitzer who was on duty at Papa's left, the contract had no hope. Sooner or later, the Toucan would make his ♡A and fire a club back. But Papa had already perceived that the stage was set for one of his favourite deceptions. With an air of calm innocence, he ducked the trick.

Suddenly realising that the hand might provide material for the *Griffins' Chronicle*, the callow young kibitzer hastily grabbed his E.B.U. pen.

He could see it all. Declarer would capture the second round of diamonds, draw trumps, finishing on the table, and discard his singleton ♡J on the ◇K. Then, a ruffing finesse against East, would establish three heart winners on which he could discard his long diamonds.

The deal had 'front page' written all over it, goggled the

C.Y.K. He might even get a by-line.

But alas, *Rabbit Bites Papa* had long ceased to be front page news. R.R. was pondering the significance of the Toucan's signals. The ◇10 could mean anything, and probably did. But he was beginning to have second thoughts about that extravagant jack of clubs.

Then he saw it – it was a classic McKenney, demanding a heart switch. And R.R., the strong man of the partnership, had nearly missed it! Belatedly, he switched to a heart, and his partner's club return defeated Papa by two tricks.

When O.O. recommended Papa for the coveted prize, his speech to the committee was constructed to avoid maligning the players concerned.

"Papa's fine effort failed for a most unusual reason," he vouchsafed. "For the first time in the club's bizarre history, a discouraging signal was mistaken for a McKenney for the *higher* ranking suit. He therefore qualifies for the Lord Tennyson award for Gallant Failure. Gallant, you ask? And well you may. But remember that Themistocles Papadopoulos knew that he had perished because someone had blundered. Yet his only thought was to give the blunderers a priceless lesson in signalling. His colourful invective does not diminish the unselfishness of his action. They now know that when playing HDLE, McKenney signals are also inverted, a discovery which is bound to make a tremendous contribution to the success of their partnership."

A Message to Dummy

Papa's second Oscar-winning performance came later in the same rubber. At game all, R.R. and T.T. had made a part score of thirty at their fourth attempt, when the Toucan dealt the following hand.

North/South Game and 30. Dealer North.

T.T.
♠ A43
♡ 654
♢ KQJ10
♣ KQ2

Karapet

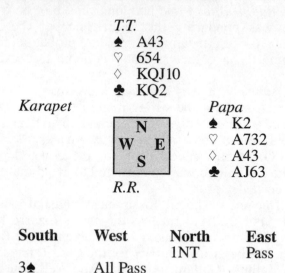

Papa
♠ K2
♡ A732
♢ A43
♣ AJ63

R.R.

South	West	North	East
		1NT	Pass
3♠	All Pass		

Karapet led the ♡J to Papa's ace, and when R.R. dropped the ♡K, there seemed little hope for the defence from East's point of view. Declarer surely held six trumps, and with dummy's minor suit holdings he should lose no more than a trick in each suit.

So Papa bent his sharp, devious mind to the task of finding an irresistible defence to an immovable contract, and perceived one slender chance.

Glancing round at the kibitzers, he switched to the ♣3. If Karapet's card forced out one of dummy's honours, the Greek would be poised for one of his pet coups: under the ♠A, he would unblock his king, hoping against hope that his partner held the queen, an entry which would enable him to fire through a second club. He could hardly wait to see the look on the Hog's face, when he heard about it.

This was the full deal:

T.T.
♠ A43
♡ 654
◇ KQJ10
♣ KQ2

Karapet
♠ Q10
♡ J1098
◇ 9852
♣ 954

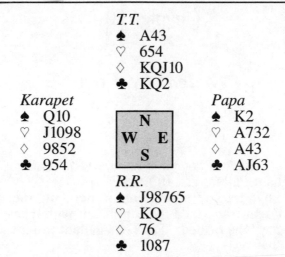

Papa
♠ K2
♡ A732
◇ A43
♣ AJ63

R.R.
♠ J98765
♡ KQ
◇ 76
♣ 1087

Amazingly, on the club switch, the Rabbit smartly produced the ♣10, and when trumps broke favourably, not even he could fail to make nine tricks.

Papa threw down his cards in exasperation, not at the loss of the rubber, but the pain of seeing the destruction of his spectacular unblocking play.

"What possessed you to go up with that killing ten of clubs?" he demanded.

"Perhaps I am not as bad as you think I am," replied the Rabbit with dignity. "In this situation the eight could mean anything. Why it could be low from a doubleton, or a singleton. My ten told Timothy that I had three worthless cards."

"Worthless?" spluttered Papa.

"Well, er, I suppose they turned out to be useful, the way it went." The Rabbit didn't care to pursue the point. Papa was usually such a careful defender and he didn't want to draw attention to a fine player's Toucan-like blunder.

"But why in the name of Sanity did you want to give information to dummy?" protested the incredulous Greek.

"It's our new signalling method, HDLE. We may have had a success with it a few hands ago, but we need all the practice we can get."

Chapter 20

Ordeal by Fire

"Tell me, Sir," asked a boyish student. "What is the difference between Gallant Failure and Ill Luck?"

Stunned by the appalling ignorance of the younger generation, Oscar transfixed the supplicant with a basilisk eye.

"Elementary," he rasped. "Papa has gallant failures; Karapet has ill luck."

The Armenian's case had posed a problem so utterly insoluble that only the Owl could solve it. How could Karapet be given an award when, since 1423, it had been rendered impossible for a Djoulikyan to win anything?

"Thank you for your forty-seven unlucky hands," he told Karapet. "But before we had time to judge them, they were destroyed by what appears to have been an act of spontaneous combustion."

Karapet, the only man in the Western Galactic Quadrant who would have believed him, groaned fatalistically. "I expected no less," he muttered darkly. "The same thing happened to the forty-seven copies I kept at home."

"I'm sorry to tell you, Karapet, that this means we cannot award the medal until the next millennium," regretted Oscar.

"I shall be ready," Karapet assured him.

"However, as there were no other worthy entries, we would like you to accept our worst wishes for the future, together with the cracked Georgian mirror."

"Will you have it mended?" pleaded Karapet poignantly.

"Of course. Now, and on every future occasion when it spontaneously cracks, as it undoubtedly will. Meanwhile, please accept this framed diagram of the unkindest cut of all."

As he gazed at his unluckiest hand, Karapet looked more contentedly morose than ever, and a tear rolled happily down the long Djoulikyan nose.

Game All. Dealer South.

T.T.
♠ K5
♡ 65
◇ QJ109765
♣ 53

Ch.Ch.
♠ 7
♡ J98
◇ A43
♣ J109872

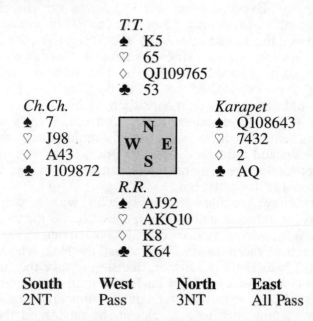

Karapet
♠ Q108643
♡ 7432
◇ 2
♣ AQ

R.R.
♠ AJ92
♡ AKQ10
◇ K8
♣ K64

South	West	North	East
2NT	Pass	3NT	All Pass

When the Chimp led the ♣J, the Rabbit, remembering tip number seven from his favourite book, learnedly studied the dummy. It didn't help him much, but it gave Karapet time to plan a spectacular defence. Realising that to beat the contract he would need to find partner with a top diamond, he played the ♣Q to the first trick.

A more worthy declarer, discounting the chances of a four-four club break when the queen appeared, would probably have ducked the opening lead. But the hapless Rabbit took with the king and laid down the ◇K, which the Chimp ducked. Karapet, sensing that immortality was only seconds away, was trembling with excitement. When his partner took the second round, he would unblock the ♣A, hopefully leaving the way clear for Charlie to cash a large number of that suit. Such coups had been performed before, but never by a Djoulikyan, or not since 31st October, 1932, when the Witch was celebrating Halloween by a dalliance with a distant warlock. Nothing, but nothing, could possibly go wrong.

But when R.R. went into an ominous trance, Karapet

shuddered. Was the meddlesome G.A. about to desecrate his work of art? Expecting the worst, he was not disappointed. Unaccountably abandoning diamonds, the Rabbit crossed to the ♠K, finessed the ♠J and cashed the ♠A. When the queen and ten failed to appear, he had a shrewd suspicion that his ♠9 was not a master, so he cashed his top hearts. The welcome sight of the Chimp's knave established the ♡10 as declarer's ninth trick.

"You didn't need my diamonds then," smiled T.T.

"No, Timothy," explained R.R. "You see, I knew after the first trick that Charlie had a fistful of winning clubs, and when someone ducked the first diamond I guessed he was rectifying the count for a squeeze against declarer. So the majors were my best bet, only fifty-fifty, but ..."

"Fifty-fifty?" wailed Karapet, who was a world-class authority on the odds against lost causes. "It was thirteen-to-one against. Why, why, why does this always happen to me?"

"What R.R. meant to say," intervened the Hog, who had been watching, "was that after his, er, decision to take the first trick, the only chance was to play Charlie for long clubs and you for the ace. When your diamond deuce appeared, bearing an uncanny resemblance to a singleton, he envisaged the actual layout. Knowing that a master of your calibre would find that venerable unblocking play, he was forced to adopt an unusual line. As you know, explaining his genius is not his forte, but I am quite willing to be a Bosworth to his Johnson."

As he cut the Armenian as his partner for the next rubber, he decided that a kind word would be a wise investment.

"But you have my sympathy, Karapet. If Constable had been a Djoulikyan, it would have rained burning pitch before the paint had dried on his *Fighting Téméraire*."

Chapter 21

The Glittering Prizes

"Ready when you are, Mr De Mille," quipped the Corgi to the Owl.

Every club has its childish element, and though in the case of the Griffins the epithet applied to a mere nine-tenths of the membership, it was inevitable that the presentation of the Millennium Awards, on New Years Eve, should become known as the Oscar Ceremonies.

The Corgi's disappointment when he was told that he hadn't won anything vanished when O.O. invited him to co-host. Having watched many Academy Award evenings, he admired the way the famous presenters paid tribute to the winners, subtly allowing their cynical contempt to peep through a superficial veneer of respect.

There was standing room only in the main card room as Oscar presented the first major award.

"It has been facetiously claimed that our primary objective on a bridge hand is to win the post-mortem," he perorated. "I regard this not as a jest but a truism. Bridge is the greatest of games because everybody is a winner. When we lose at chess we cannot bemoan the luck of the deal or the lie of the cards. In a golf tournament we have no partner to blame, and our caddy is a poor substitute. Moreover, in bridge most bids and plays are a matter, not of mathematics, but opinion. Put these facts together and we see that the post-mortem is the perfect forum for excusing our failures, redressing our grievances, shifting blame to our partners, and turning humiliating defeats into glorious victories."

He was about to continue in the same vein, when he noticed that several of his junior kibitzers were not only glancing at their watches, but shaking them to see if they were still running. Reluctantly, he discarded his prompt cards covering the history of contract bridge, and plunged into his finale.

"It is with great pride that I announce the winner of the prize for Persistence in the post-mortem, for she has never lost one. She is, of course, the unsinkable Molly Mule."

As Molly marched forward, someone clapped. After glancing towards the door to see who had entered, she was so choked with emotion that she was forced to cut her acceptance speech to a bare ten minutes.

Oscar gave a heavily censored version of a deal which exemplified Molly's talent, even though she was dummy. The uncensored version follows:

Papa, West, had been faced with this lead problem:

    ♠ A1043
    ♡ J62
    ◇ A42
    ♣ Q97

His right hand opponent, the Secretary Bird, had dealt and opened one spade. The auction, which was unusually informative, proceeded as follows:

South	West	North	East
1♠	Pass	2♡	Pass
3♠	Pass	3NT	Pass
4♠	All Pass		

Papa could see three tricks in his own hand, and normally he would look no further than a small diamond as his opening lead. However, the club suit offered the best prospect for a fourth trick, and the suit lent itself to a pretty deception. Without hesitation, he selected the *queen* of clubs. It had the unusual merit of being both flamboyant and sensible. If partner had the ace or king, it wouldn't matter which card was led. Whereas if she held the jack ...

The full hand was exactly what he hoped for:

East/West Game. Dealer South.

M.M.
♠ —
♡ A109854
◇ K65
♣ K1064

Papa
♠ A1043
♡ J62
◇ A42
♣ Q97

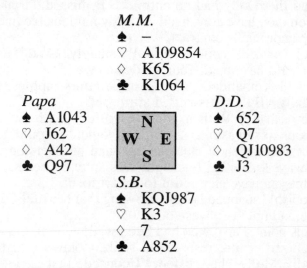

D.D.
♠ 652
♡ Q7
◇ QJ10983
♣ J3

S.B.
♠ KQJ987
♡ K3
◇ 7
♣ A852

The Secretary Bird captured with his ace and produced the ♠Q. Papa took the trick and put declarer under immediate pressure by continuing with the ♣7. S.B. played the ten from the table and, when Dolly won and returned a diamond for Papa to give her a club ruff, the contract was two off.

Molly, who had been smouldering since halfway through the auction, sprang into attack with a series of bewildering pincer movements.

"Four hearts was the contract," she sniffed. "But obviously you like the challenge of playing in a six-nil fit."

"How could I guess you had rebid no trumps with a void in my suit?" demanded S.B.

"Well if you hadn't been so determined to hog the contract, you would have discovered that three no trumps also happens to make."

"But I didn't know about your magnificent triple stop in diamonds," sneered S.B.

"No sweat. I would have ducked the diamond lead. Even if I never take a trick in the suit, the contract makes. I run the ten of hearts to West's jack and can later knock out his spade ace," countered Molly, who had, quite fortuitously, stumbled upon the winning strategy.

"Of course, silly of me not to realize that diamonds were six-three and that Dolly had no entry," S.B. hissed. "I take my hat off to you, you have conceived a highly implausible line to make a highly improbable contract."

"But it worked," countered Molly smugly. "And if I'd been in your seat, I'd have made four spades as well."

"How?" demanded S.B., his Adam's apple throbbing homicidally. "By a cross-ruff, I suppose."

"A cross-ruff? With a void?" scoffed M.M., who was as impervious to sarcasm as she was to logic. "I would never have fallen for that queen of clubs lead. It had whiskers on it."

"I always knew that hindsight was an exact science," sighed S.B. "But you have elevated it to an art form."

"Rubbish!" snapped Molly, showing that her lifelong study of repartee had not been wasted.

At this point, Papa, who had been wallowing in the sulk of an unrecognized genius, resolved to strike a blow for justice.

"Really, Molly," he scoffed. "I concede that during the later stages of play the lead of the queen from my holding is not unknown, but at trick one it can hardly be an everyday occurrence." He winked knowingly at the kibitzers. "Except at the Mermaids, of course."

"You see, Dolly?" Molly turned jubilantly to her fellow Mermaid. "Whenever men are losing an argument to a woman, they resort to sexist comments." She cut the cards towards Papa with a victorious thump. "When they should be dealing."

A Tribute to Walter

After Molly had reclaimed her seat to a deafening silence, the Corgi rose.

"When I tell you that the next prize is a late-Victorian abacus, you will know that the winner is that wizard of single-digit arithmetic, Walter Walrus. If it is true that a man may be taken prisoner by thought, we can say with confidence that W.W. has never been captured. By his unselfish devotion to the cause of point-counting and signalling, he has abolished the need for painful cerebral activity, not just for himself, but for everyone at his table. To play with him takes us back to those salad days, when we too were as innocent as a new-laid egg."

He waited respectfully to allow an ancient Griffin to wipe away a tear.

"To play against him is a rest cure. From his bidding, his metronomic signalling and his guileless demeanour, we soon know his hand as well as we know our own and dummy's. That is why we can produce those far-sighted declarer plays for which the Griffins are justly famous. It is no wonder that Walter, the unsung hero of those coups, is the most popular opponent in Clubland, and the worthy recipient of the award for Mastery of the Milton Work Point Count."

Walter bowed to the audience with all the dignity a man with a sixty-inch waist could muster. He seized the abacus and caressed the beads lovingly.

Then he started to count them.

A Tale of Two Commas

"I must applaud your crisis management," murmured Peregrine Penguin.

"Thank you," replied the Owl. "We came through that one by the skin of our teeth."

The committee had secretly reinstated the Best Play by a Lady category, and it had been secretly won by Dolly the Dove. If Molly the Mule found out, violence would be inevitable, bloodshed probable, and loss of life a good outside bet.

Oscar had solved the problem by sandwiching Dolly between the two jurisprudence awards, won by the Secretary Bird, for upholding the laws, and by the Chimp, for bending them. Meanwhile Charlie tempted Molly with a champagne celebration in the bar, and the even greater inducement of missing S.B.'s acceptance speech.

Now there was a further difficulty for the organisers. As Papa had refused to attend the ceremony, the Owl and the Corgi cut to decide who should excuse his absence to a curious audience. The Corgi lost.

"In the latest issue of the *Griffins' Chronicle*," explained O.O., "an unfortunate statement appeared."

He switched on the overhead projector to display the

following sentence:

Papa admits H.H. is the best player in the club

"I have a letter from Mr Papadopoulos' solicitors," proceeded Oscar. "They maintain that their client said no such thing, and that to suggest that he did so is a slur on his character, his sanity and his reputation as a bridge expert."

He paused for three blinks, an enigmatic hoot and a sip of whisky and water.

"I looked into the incident," he went on, gazing severely at a junior kibitzer who was trying to crawl under a chair. "It appeared that the sub-editor concerned was absent from school the day they taught punctuation. The sentence should have read somewhat differently."

He changed the transparency for one which revealed:

Papa, admits H.H., is the best player in the club

"Naturally, I asked H.H. to confirm that he made the remark, and I understand that he wishes to say a few words on the subject. And I hope 'few' is the operative word," he murmured optimistically.

The Hog rose with imperious humility. "I freely acknowledge both the remark and the amended punctuation," he declared, to gasps of astonishment. "Halfway through our recent friendly match, Themistocles was trailing, and his morale was low. So for the sake of the game, I decided that he needed a psychological boost."

In the silence which followed, we could have heard a pin drop, and when Dolly the Dove chose that moment to drop one, H.H. patiently waited for the echoes to subside.

"I realised that by paying him that compliment I was placing kindness above truth, and sportsmanship above accuracy. But in the immortal words of Brigitte Bardot: '*je ne regret rien*'. My sacrifice was not in vain, for Themistocles rallied valiantly, and my team's final victory, against some world-class opposition, was so close that I believe we can all look forward to a return match on similar terms."

He waited for applause but, seeing that his fellow Griffins

preferred, for some strange reason, to sit in mute reverence, he ploughed on serenely:

"I have added my endorsement to the club's carefully punctuated letter of apology," he informed them. "It would be a tragedy if, through losing two commas, we also lost a member whose losses show that he prizes boldness, optimism, ingenuity and originality far above sordid financial gain."

"And the third best player in the club," broke in Sophia the Siren, loyally supporting her quasi-distant relative, and exacting an embarrassed squeak from the club's quasi number two.

The Corgi grinned. Good fellow that he was, he looked forward to making sure that, when Themistocles returned, he would hear about his cousin's extravagant compliment.

Chapter 22

The Loose Ends

The first half of the Oscar ceremonies was brought to a climax by the entry of an armoured column of waiters bearing refills, and the award for All-Round Brilliance. It had been won when Beppo Walenski's tenacious attempts to make his five club contract were thwarted by the Hog and the Rabbit.

O.O. read out a note, penned by the Chimp in a convincing facsimile of Walenski's handwriting. As he had forsaken bridge for the sanctuary of a Trappist monastery, the risk was small.

Dear Griffins,

I would be honoured to receive the coveted award, but I feel that it rightly belongs to my favourite partner, Timothy Toucan. Although he was dummy at the time, without his inspiration, not to mention his futuristic bidding, the remarkable events which followed would not have been possible.

With fond memories,

Beppo

The audience clapped as much for the sagacious Owl as the ingenuous Toucan, for who else could have devised a way of persuading Timothy to accept an award, and how else would T.T. have accepted it but by proxy?

And what else could have stopped the applause in an instant but the sight of Colin the Corgi rising to present the first of the minor awards, for such trivial qualities as individual skill.

Switching on the projector, the C.C. revealed one of the Hog's latest triumphs:

Game All. Dealer East.

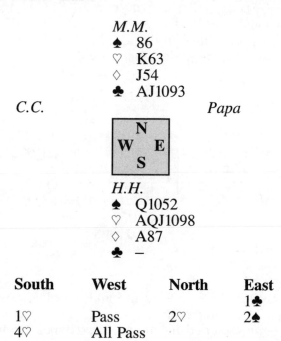

M.M.
♠ 86
♡ K63
◇ J54
♣ AJ1093

C.C.   Papa

H.H.
♠ Q1052
♡ AQJ1098
◇ A87
♣ —

South	West	North	East
			1♣
1♡	Pass	2♡	2♠
4♡	All Pass		

"I found the inspired lead of a trump," confessed the Corgi. "An optimistic declarer would see the opportunity of making ten tricks: two aces, six hearts, the queen of spades, and a spade ruff. A pessimist would see the insuperable problem of finding entries to dummy. Perhaps someone would care to suggest a solution. By the way, leading the queen of spades from hand won't work."

There was an excited buzz, while every Griffin tried in vain to find somebody who had witnessed the deal, which had been played that afternoon. Appreciating their bafflement, Colin mischievously resolved to add to it.

"As most of you will have deduced," he told them, "the answer is an end play against East at trick three." He removed the transparency, and consulted his notes. "Now our next hand is far more difficult. It involves ..."

He broke off at the request of the Rabbit, who had a question: "Excuse me, Colin, but could we see that last one again. Er,

Timothy hasn't quite grasped it yet, and Walter hasn't finished counting the points, and I'm not sure how H.H. rectified the count for the end play."

"I do apologise," smirked the Corgi. "For those of you who haven't guessed the entire deal, here it is:"

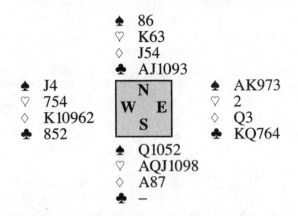

```
                    ♠ 86
                    ♡ K63
                    ◊ J54
                    ♣ AJ1093
    ♠ J4                              ♠ AK973
    ♡ 754          N                  ♡ 2
    ◊ K10962     W   E                ◊ Q3
    ♣ 852          S                  ♣ KQ764
                    ♠ Q1052
                    ♡ AQJ1098
                    ◊ A87
                    ♣ —
```

"Declarer won the first trick in hand, and laid down the ace of diamonds," C.C. told them.

"Sheer genius!" cried an unidentified voice from the back row.

"I agree with you, H.H.," acknowledged the Corgi. "On the bidding, East was likely to hold ten black cards, and almost certainly a diamond honour. When no honour dropped under the ace, the Hog opted to play for the actual distribution. He advanced a low diamond at trick three. I played low – rising with the king would have been flamboyant, but futile – and Papa was truly fixed. Whatever he returned, declarer would come to ten tricks."

He waited defiantly for a challenge, but as none was forthcoming, he continued his commentary.

"Being Papa, he was ready with a spot of low cunning, so he produced a low spade. He was rewarded with the sight of the queen landing on the table, and a pitying smile from H.H."

"I really must object, C.C." The Hog rose majestically. "It was the smile of one master to another, who has done his best. And you are making too much of my modest coup. Why, Molly the Mule had seen several like it at the Mermaids, and Papa, who is the best player in the club, by a margin of two commas, described it as routine. Now, if you really want some examples of my ..."

"Yes, yes!" intervened Oscar. "Be patient, H.H. We are about to present the individual brilliancy awards, and there is a slim outside chance that you will be mentioned again."

As the Hog returned apoplectically to his seat, O.O. took Colin's place at the projector.

"There are many more magnificent deals," proclaimed the Owl, raising aloft an imposing pile of transparencies and swiftly discarding them by popular demand. "But you will read about them soon enough. And you will marvel at the astonishing number which display the transcendental skills of H.H ... and R.R."

To forestall the Rabbit's incipient gurgle of incredulity, Oscar resumed calmly:

"I have no doubt that H.H. will tell you when, how and why he fashioned each *magnum opus*, for he has always been eager to share his thoughts with lesser mortals."

"Which means everyone," interpolated the Corgi.

"R.R. on the other hand," went on the Owl, with a censorious blink, "will explain nothing, for his flashes of genius are like bolts of lightning; their origins are lost in the ensuing thunder. Usually from the angry mouths of his hapless victims."

He took a sip of Madeira, to allow a lone hand clap from Sophia the Siren to punctuate his *bon mot*, and proceeded:

"Yet it is not our task to speculate on the nature of unpremeditated thought, but to reward it, and it is my pleasure to announce that each of the prizes for individual brilliance are shared by H.H. and R.R."

In the hiatus that followed, H.H. graciously suggested that the Rabbit should keep all the winners' certificates, and R.R. reciprocated by allowing the Hog to keep the vintage wines and the gourmet food hampers.

There wasn't a dry eye in the house.

Chapter 23

The Chimes at Midnight

As the tick-tick-tock of their stately clock reminded the Griffins that it was only five minutes to the Millennium, Oscar invited Peregrine the Penguin to propose a toast to the club.

"While we await the chimes of midnight," began P.P., "let us reflect on the Griffins' outstanding contributions to the Ascent of Man. Founded by the Master of the King's Pleasures for the entertainment of Charles II, the club's first great achievement was to redefine the laws of faro, ombre and whist, inspiring Sir Isaac Newton to begin the equally important task of redefining the Universe. In later years it was the Griffins' doctrine of the Survival of the Fittest which led Darwin to adapt the theory to certain other fields. And it was your own Hog who, long before the collapse of the Berlin Wall, single-handedly refuted the Marxian notion of statutory equality by proving that he was more equal than anyone else. Tonight, as you wonder what the next thousand years hold in store, one thing is sure: Yours will remain an exhilarating existence, while you thrill to each turn of Fortune's wheel. With this auspicious thought, I invite you to raise your glasses to the future of your famous club."

As everyone rose, the clock began to chime, while the resonant voice of Walter the Walrus counted each sonorous note.

There were thirteen!

A young kibitzer fainted. The Hog doubled, the Owl blinked, the Penguin flapped, the Rabbit reddened, the Toucan bounced, S.B. hissed, and the Corgi raised a quizzical eyebrow. Could the millennium bug have penetrated the works of an 18th century long-case clock?

Only Karapet knew the answer. It was writ in fiery letters on his Free Armenian soul.

The Witch was at it again.